ANGER IS MY FRIEND: Rethinking teen anger management

SAM ROSS

Published by Teenage Whisperer Press

First Printing, 2013

———————————————————

Teenage Whisperer

contact@teenagewhisperer.co.uk

www.teenagewhisperer.co.uk

———————————————————

ISBN: 1491041080
ISBN-13: 978-1491041086

You were always ahead of me,
you always had the first word.

CONTENTS

OVERCOMING THE CHALLENGE OF
DISENGAGEMENT

MOVING ON

ACKNOWLEDGMENTS

Without the unwavering support, emotionally and financially of my husband, Ed, the whole Teenage Whisperer project and this book could not exist. Although he did not write it, he undoubtedly helped to create it. I will forever be grateful for this and the faith he has always shown in me.

My daughter, Annabel, who is far off the teenage years, has had to watch me juggle this, work and play. I hope she looks back and thinks I got the balance right and can appreciate that in my endeavour to help others, I was more whole myself, and consequently more wholly there for her.

Without every single young person I have worked with, I would know very little. Theory and academic training has taught me some, young people have taught me a whole load more, not least to open my eyes, ears and heart to their struggles. I hope that in this book I am serving them well.

INTRODUCTION:
THE ANGER RETHINK

Yet another book on anger? How dull. What is there possibly left to say that hasn't been covered by the umpteen other ones? Well I'd like to think that what you are about to read is going to bring something different, something rock-face real and something thought-provoking to the table.

Another formulaic book with generic solutions to a wholly ungeneric emotion, you probably do not need. Another book that talks clinically about anger like you might talk about an in-growing toe nail is not required either. Nor a book that dissects and analyses anger so much that you forget that it was ever attached to a human.

Anger is one of the rawest and most complex of human emotions and should be treated as such. It has roots that run deep and strong and no one-size fits all approach will work when trying to deal with it. It is precisely because anger is so strongly entwined within the person in which it inhabits that any approach that loses the person and tries to treat the anger will always ultimately fail.

If this book does one thing I want it to be this: that teens struggling with this emotion are seen. Not an anger management problem that needs to be sorted, but people, first and foremost. People who are just as prone to personal frailty as you or I, with the added complication of adolescent hormones and a world that tends to prefer to see them as problems rather than vulnerable people in crisis.

We have to see the *individual* teen if we are to have any hope of helping them make the necessary changes in their lives. We have to see the individual teen if we want to understand their very personal anger and help them disentangle themselves from it, to help them to be able to breathe, to be able to grow. It's all about relationship, about communication, about exchange.

So coming from this point I'm afraid I can't offer you a program of work to cure angry teens, abracadabra, job done. Such a thing does not and cannot exist. Good programs of work do exist, written by many skilled practitioners in the field (visit *www.teenagewhisperer.co. uk/teenanger* for examples), but they are only good when delivered within the context of a trusting relationship, where the young person has spoken and you have listened and tailored the program personally for them.

And this is the part that so many books and programs miss out. The part that can be fraught with the most challenges and difficulties. The part where you try and build that relationship. The part where you are trying to understand who they really are, what they are about. The part where you try and get them to engage. This is the gap I hope to at least partially fill.

My offering is a collection of writings to reflect upon, for you to colonise, to own, to question, to consider- in your pursuit of relationship with teens first, and in your pursuit to help them deal with their anger better, second, and in this order always.

Some chapters are written in the voice of a teen, offering insight into some of their thought patterns. The others are written in my voice and are based on my experience of working with struggling teens in education and legal youth justice systems.

In all, I hope that this book is written in an accessible, readable, thought-provoking way. You can dip in and dip out as the need takes you. It is best viewed as a collection of my reflections for you to reflect on. This can be done individually or as part of group supervision or training. It does have many practical tips and tools you can employ if you see fit, but they won't always work and they won't always be the best course of action for a particular teen.

I do not have all the answers. I don't have all the questions either. What I do have is a profound faith in your ability, realised or yet to be realised, to discern what is best for the teens in front of you, their uniqueness, their challenges, their potential, if you truly listen to them.

For this reason this book isn't intended to be a manual, more of a fertilizer, to help you in your uniqueness be the best help to your teens in their uniqueness. This is where genuine relationship grows and great practice flourishes. It is not found step-by-step in the pages in a book, but in the gentle imbibing of new ideas and suggestions that feed your own professional creativity and desire to constantly be better at reaching out, at connecting.

So go read, see, hear, go connect and go guiding. It's the best, most effective anger management intervention going.

STAYING CONNECTED

This book started its life as a handful of blog posts on the Teenage Whisperer website, *www.teenagewhisperer.co.uk*

The website with its blog and resource pages aims to help all those who work with teens become teenage whisperers- people who can relate to, understand and help teenagers break out of negative behaviour cycles so that they can truly flourish. Its focus is very much on the practical business of engaging the most challenging teens. If you like what you read here then chances are you'll like what you read on the website too!

The free downloadable resources that are referred to in the book, along with suggested further reading can be found at: *www.teenagewhisperer.co.uk/teenanger*

I have a fantastic troup of followers on Facebook and Twitter and we regularly interact with each other providing support and resource ideas. I also regularly post the latest news items and research findings that are relevant to working with teenagers. Please join us.

www.facebook.com/teenagewhisperer

twitter.com/Teen_Whisperer

-
WHAT ON EARTH IS GOING
ON WITH THEM?
-

ANGER IS MY FRIEND

You probably don't realise this, but anger is my friend. My best friend. It's my certainty amidst uncertainty. It's always there for me, it protects me. It tells me I'm alive. It shows me that I exist in other people's worlds. And you know what? It often makes me feel good, real good. It shows I have some power, some real raw power within me and I don't get that any other time. For those few moments I can be king of the world and no-one can take that from me.

It's my emotional rock in a sea of mixed up feelings that I have no way of understanding or processing. I love my Mum but she's crap. I love my Dad but he's a loser who doesn't care about me, I don't even know where he is. I really like some of my teachers and we can have a bit of a laugh. But I'm scared, really scared that maybe they'll get too close and see how vulnerable I am. Or my mates will think I'm pathetic for getting on with them so well. Or my Mum will be angry and think that I'm trying to replace her or something. Or maybe they'll end up finding me annoying and will reject me.

I don't know how to express all this, I'm not even aware of

most of it. I need to express something, and as my head is whirring with all these thoughts I seem to have no control over and don't fit in my head, I end up blowing my top- I get angry. Me being angry with me for having such conflicting thoughts. Me being angry with you for making me feel this way with your kindness, your nagging, basically whatever you do.

So amidst this blur of conflicting emotions I have a rock, a default feeling I can fall back on, one I can easily express even when all the others are confused. Even though it looks like my storm, it's not, it's my safe port. My anger, my best friend.

It protects me. It wraps me in ten layers of bubble-wrap and no amount of popping is going to let you get to me. Deep down I do want you to see my pain and my conflicting emotions and help me process them but I'm scared, so if I sense you're getting too close I will push you away. I will find a reason to erupt, a reason for me to hate you and a reason for you to run.

I don't want to expose myself to the risk of being hurt or rejected again. I'm terrified that you'll see the real me, will think I'm crazy, will be shocked, completely horrified. So I'll erect my big fat anger diversion sign and send you off down the road where you can dump me. It leaves me to sit in my bubble-wrap, protected from the world once more. My anger, my friend.

The thing is I know exactly what to expect from you if I blow up. It's beautifully predictable. I push you away, you push me away. It's my certainty amidst my emotional chaos. I control the end result. I might not be in control of my head but this I am in control of. My anger, my steady friend.

Anger also makes me feel alive. When I get that sick feeling in my stomach, or my face feels hot and flushed and my heart is beating like a high-speed train I know that I live. I feel like such a nobody that sometimes I wonder if I exist. But when those anger juices start pumping I am in no doubt. I don't feel like a shell of a person any more, I don't feel empty. So my anger fills me, it fills my void. Where security, stability, love, happiness, self-worth and purpose should live, there lives my anger. I'll take anger over emptiness any day. My anger knows I live.

And when I get a reaction from you I know I exist, not just in my own skin, but I exist in your world too. I make it onto your radar. And wow, that gives me a buzz. I might feel stupid and embarrassed after, further adding to my confused feelings, but at the time it feels great. Hell, I actually have some power for once. I *really* do exist.

To see you getting angry right back at me, to see you squirm when I hurl an insult, to see you struggle to regain control, to see you have to call for backup; it shows I have some influence. It shows I can make people notice and think about me.

It shows I can make people do what I want them to, like chuck me out of the classroom when I really can't do the work and don't want everyone to see that; to make you push me away if I feel you are getting too close; to make you stop talking about that thing that really upsets me. And you know what one of the cleverest parts of me being angry is? I can make you feel what I feel. I can make you feel insecure, frustrated, vulnerable, useless, scared, out of control, confused. I can show you the friends of my anger. My anger, my best friend.

You should also know that feeling this power is addictive. Some people get addicted to drugs or alcohol to make them feel better, others to exercise, others to food, some to combinations of things. Well my primary addiction is my anger. It works for me on so many levels, or so it seems. My anger, my BFF.

Which is where you come in. You've probably been 'called in' to sort out my anger, to do some 'anger management' with me. Well shove right off.

Nothing makes me more angry than someone trying to fix my anger. It's like someone coming in and telling me that I need to kill my friend. When my back is against the wall and someone tries to take one of the last friends I have then I will tell you straight- get stuffed. You don't mess with me and you don't mess with my best mate.

If you really want to help me, you need to treat my anger for the friend it is. So just like you don't tell me not to do something cos you know it'll make me do it more, don't tell me to quit my anger cos it'll only push us closer together. What you've got to do is help me come to realise that the way my anger friend treats me isn't helping me in life, that I am actually held hostage by it and that there are better friends out there for me, other options. You then leave it to me to decide.

Cos the truth is that my anger actually chokes me when it has this addictive hold over me. Although I can be really noisy with it, it actually stops me from speaking and stops me from being really heard. It stops me from being able to properly connect with people and to even try to begin to explain myself and my feelings. It steals my emotional voice. It shoves a rag in my mouth and raps tape round my face.

So you've got to help me see this and this is no easy job. As you try to connect with me, my anger pushes back and tries to keep you out, stopping you from helping me. So expect a lot of angry outbursts from me at first. Get used to being told to 'fuck off'. Desensitise yourself to it. I don't really deep down mean it, this is my anger talking.

After a while me and my anger realise that you are not going away. That my anger doesn't always work at pushing you away. And then it will dawn on me that maybe my anger isn't that powerful after all. It might work well at getting me what I need at a particular moment, like you to get lost, or to make you feel like me, but it doesn't actually get me what I really want and need- a secure attachment to someone. A relationship with someone who I can really talk to, who I feel safe enough with to explore my emotional conflicts and confusion. And the thing is that as soon as I actually start talking about all this pent-up confusion, I gradually, bit by bit lose my reliance on my friend, my anger. Me and my friend begin to separate, our explosive relationship diminishes.

Once my anger with you loses its hold, I have a bit of room to breathe, room to explore my anger with everything and everyone else. I can then explore how I use anger to protect myself, to ensure predictability in how others treat me and then look for alternative ways of protecting myself.

I then might get to a place where I can begin to unwrap some of the excess layers of bubble-wrap around me so that I have the confidence to take the risk of 'putting myself out there' a bit more. I will then come to see that if I reveal more of myself to others, then we will better connect and my basic need for attachment will be met. I need to learn that emotional attachment doesn't have to be scary and negative, as it may have been in the past, and the benefits make it a risk worth taking.

Part of just talking with you will do that, it will be my first test-run at this. Next steps could be sharing with others like me who have made some progress in understanding their best friend, a sort of anger support group. We can then begin to share with others who 'get it'. I'll end up with some good mates this way who I really connect with which will further meet my base need for meaningful attachment. So rather than a bunch of 'angry mess-ups' in a room together being a recipe for disaster as adults so often think, it can really help us. We can find each other as friends and we can support each other. We can tell our destructive, disengaging anger 'friends' to take a hike.

You can help us prepare and cope with the unpredictability of life so we don't go nuts when things don't go our way, or how we expected them to. We won't then need to resort to the predictability of an anger exchange to try and regain control. Show us how spontaneity can be a good thing and that we don't need to be in complete control the whole time.

Validate our feelings of anger. We so often get told that our anger is wrong. Problem is that it is a huge part of us so telling us it is just plain wrong invalidates us. It's not our anger that is wrong, it is the way we inappropriately express it in the wrong situations. Help us to also see that often when we are angry it is not the situation in front of us that we are angry at, but something much deeper.

And this is where looking at our triggers in-depth helps. It helps us work this out. But you don't just help me discover what my triggers are, but also why they are my triggers. Once you help me do this then disentangling appropriate from inappropriate responses becomes much easier.

So 'anger management' doesn't have to involve completely kicking my good friend anger to the curb. He is a valid friend who does have a place in my life. I just have to make sure that he doesn't take over, doesn't control me, turns up for the right events in the right clothing and doesn't mess up my thinking and my actions.

My anger can be a particularly good friend in one area. When controlled by me and used appropriately, he can help me seek proper justice for events in my life. That is often why I am so angry- I'm angry at the injustice of things that have happened and happen to me. Problem is, in trying to voice my anger, I often direct it at the wrong person and in the wrong way. Show me how to do this the right way.

I can seek justice with my anger for events like being abused and reporting the perpetrator and ensuring it never happens again. Or seek justice for the little things, like getting angry that my worker never shows up on time and doesn't seem to care. Show me how to channel that anger into making an appropriate complaint. Help me to get justice by communicating in a way that gets the change I need. When I see positive results I am unlikely to turn to my destructive friend so regularly.

So help me turn my destructive, controlling, life-encompassing angry best friend into a positive, life-building, life-changing friend that only comes round when he's really needed. The process won't be easy, and I'll have my relapses, but I can get there.

Just remember that whenever talking to me or my mates about our anger, don't disrespect our friend and what we feel he does for us. Just help us see how he oversteps the mark and messes stuff up for us. Then we will put anger back in his place and change his role in our lives. We have a lot to be angry about, and its usually not the surface stuff you see. Help us harness the real root of our anger and help us use it for own and others' benefit. Make what seems like a bad friend, into something good.

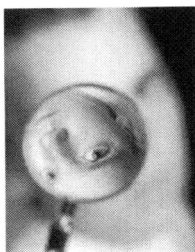

WHEN YOU SEE MORE THAN YOU SEE

When I smash a chair, I'm not just smashing a chair. I'm expressing my *frustration*. My frustration at not being able to do the work; my frustration at not being able to read; my frustration at feeling stupid; my frustration at feeling like you made me look small in front of my mates; my frustration at the fact that I've had to move from my foster carer's again; my frustration that my Dad uses me as his punch bag; my frustration that my Mum had to die; my frustration that there's never any money; my frustration that no-one cares; my frustration at being useless.

When I yell and scream and call you a 'fucking cow' or 'dick', I'm not just yelling and screaming at you. I'm building a *defence*. A defence against my vulnerability; a defence against being exposed; a defence against my great shame; a defence against my great well of hurt. I'm building a fort of invective that I can hide in. I'm defending myself against your perceived assault. You may have no idea what you said or did, sometimes even I don't know really. All I know is that something deep within me was triggered and survival mode kicked in, and I'm fighting for my life. And I'm making myself look as big as I can in the hope that you won't see how very small I feel.

When I punch a hole in the wall, I'm not just punching a hole in the wall. I'm giving you something else to look at. The wall is a *diversion*, my avoidance. It diverts your attention, it diverts mine. Away from having to deal with the shame I feel for having been in trouble in the first place. Away from having to think, once more, what a failure I am. Away from having to listen once more about what a disappointment I am. Away from having to address why I behaved in a particular way in the first place. Away from having to consider my frustration. Away from having to acknowledge my deep-running emotions, my deep-running pain. At the rejection, the abuse, the loss, the neglect, the feeling that I really don't matter. Me avoiding addressing the real issues, me making damn sure you don't get any closer to the truth. So focus on the damage to the wall and I'll keep my damage to myself.

When I deliberately smash a mug on the ground, I'm not just smashing a mug to the ground. As it hits the ground and loudly splinters into a million pieces, everyone looks, I have their *attention*. The spotlight falls on me... I am noticed. Noticed in a world where I don't exist to my parents, except as an inconvenience; noticed in a world where no one seems to have clocked that I am being bullied; noticed in a world where I am used as someone's sexual play thing; noticed when all the attention falls on a more favoured or illness-afflicted sibling; noticed when I am an invisible carer for my alcoholic parent and an invisible surrogate mother or father for my kid sisters; noticed when no-one seems to realise that this constant moving from foster carer to children's home and being split up from my brother is killing me from the inside. I'll take attention for a smashed mug over no attention at all any day.

When I smash up my room so that everything straight is bent, everything whole is now in pieces, I am not just smashing up my room. I am visually and physically expressing how *overwhelmed* I am. I don't know what to do with myself. I am so frustrated, so stressed, I have lost it. I've been walking on a knife-edge and the knife has now got me. I'm not trying to make a statement, not trying to get my own way by inflicting as much damage as I can. I have simply lost it, my brain doesn't know what to do other than direct me to release some of this tension physically before my head literally explodes. Explodes and my feelings of inadequacy or my dirtiness or my feelings of being unloved or exploited splatter themselves everywhere for all to see. So I physically explode. It's easier to tidy up this mess than the mess of my feelings.

When I punch that girl, I'm not just punching her. It's not so much about hurting her, it's about the adrenaline buzz, it's about feeling big, it's about feeling her flesh against my fist. It's about *feeling something*. I'm so numb, so disconnected from myself. This way I can check I'm still actually alive. I'm hurting so deeply, so profoundly that I have not just suppressed these feelings, I've suppressed all emotions. I rarely experience joy, sadness, disappointment or excitement on the surface of my skin. I'm like a doll that has rock hard skin and just opens and closes its eyes. Just like that doll, it seems like I have no heart. I don't really experience anything. I'm there but I'm not. And in those moments when my flesh meets theirs and I experience pain, I feel the warmth of blood, bodily contact on my terms, I feel something. Not as much as most would, but I feel a little bit of something. Just enough to remind me that I am more than a doll, a robot.

When I bully and rob that kid, when I make him handover his money, his phone, when I make him beg not to be hit, I am not just bullying and robbing that kid. I am being

King and I am in *control*. I am the Master manipulator. I am as cool as a cucumber, real rage is not written on my face, but an anger lurks within me that I have dealt with, or so I think. At some point I have been on the other end. I have been controlled by someone, I have lost control. This has made me angry, this has shamed me, this has robbed me of my dignity and I was powerless to do anything about it. So I came up with my own solution- to be in control whenever I could. To somehow redress the balance. You took my control so I'll redress the balance by taking someone else's. I'll plug the gap, fill the hole within me by putting a hole in someone else.

When I post a malicious lie on Facebook about that girl, I'm not just posting a lie. I am expressing my dislike of what she did. I'm exacting *revenge*. I am showing her she cannot treat me that way and expect to get away with it. I didn't say anything at the time to her face, I didn't directly blow up in her face like Stacey did, but I'll show her.

When I threaten a lad for bumping into me as he walks past, I'm not just being menacing; I am looking for someone to have a go at. If it wasn't him it would have been someone else. I am letting off a bit of steam, stopping my pot of *resentment* from completely boiling over. Everyone's a dick, fact. Life is shit. I'm pissed off with everyone and everything so excuse me if I'm in your face, that's just life and I want everyone to know about it, and that includes you.

When you see more than you see, you see how to help me. You see what my real issue is, you see beyond the expression of my anger to the reasons behind it. You see that my anger isn't generic and that it's personal, deeply personal to me. If you want me to let go of it, you have to see what purpose it serves for me, consciously and sub-consciously and help me meet that need in another way, or help me to see life differently so that the need is no longer there. But you have to see more than you see- my motivations, my emotions and my thoughts. The roots of my actions run deeper than you think.

THE FAMILY LINE

Out of the station it pulls, ready for another outing, the anger train, chugging along the family line. Calling at Impatience, Frustration, Narcissism, Negativity, Control, Manipulation and Despair with special call-stops along the way, on request.

Come along for the ride family members! Board at any station; don't miss out on the full experience. At first you might feel like you've got on the wrong train, but before long you'll be right in the swing of things with a frequent rider loyalty card. You'll know all the stops like the back of your hand. Travelling on this train, all day, every day will soon seem normal. You won't know there are other trains, other lines. This train will become your world.

Remember, there will be some bespoke refuel stops on the way. We'll stop at school and Mr Jensen's office for some top quality diesel for you, at Sleeplessness for your Mum, at the Fairground of Memories of Malicious Negative Family Comments for your Dad, the Off-Licence for anyone who cares to drink, the Drug Dealer on the corner for those with a more diverse chemical requirement and don't forget Forgotten and Ignored, for whoever. After full refuelling please be warned, this anger train chugs along at quite some rate.... Watch it go...Whoosh!

The holes in the walls, the rages, the violence;

the horrible words, the belittling, the silence;

the impatience, the energy, the cauldron of fear;

you love them, you hate them, do you want to be here?;

you're like them, you've learned it, you're all in a rage;

oh hell, how'd this happen, you're twelve years of age?

Not meant, not deliberate, it just kinda happened;

this train's out of control, the future is blackened;

the doors are locked, the train will not cease,

the noise is too much, I just want some peace;

how to get off, do I want to, do I care?

Am I like them, am I not, am I stuck with this fare?

Oh stuff this, I'm angry, I'll just stay aboard;

stick with the known, the people, the hoard;

I'll go through my life in an angry haze,

deny there's a problem till the end of my days;

I'll pull my kids on, get them on for the ride;

in amongst their anger from my issues I'll hide;

The noise, the drama will drown out the roars;
of hurt, of pain, and closing of doors;
as my options shrink, my relationships dwindle;
cos I got pulled on this train and all it did was swindle;
swindle me out of a life of connection;
the only experience, a life of rejection;

How I wish I were not on this loco-motion;
a swirling pot, uncontrolled emotion;
it fed me, fed others, it only caused pain,
this wretched, poisonous, family anger train.

So how does it stop?
How do I get off this thing?
How do I even learn that I'm on it?
Get to a place of accepting?

That although I love them,
It's safe to depart,
It isn't disloyal,
It's understanding; being smart.

Well you get the order right,
And the rest will follow,
Don't start talking about anger

Or the relationship's in shadow.

Cos I'll only think,
You're attacking them,
Blaming and pointing,
You will not condemn.

So be smart, be clever,
Just talk about kin
As a separate topic,
That's the way in.

Of how we get on,
What we are like,
The family dynamic,
Our individual and collective psych.

Of yelling and shouting,
Or others who inwardly simmer,
They're all forms of anger
Bright or low just like a dimmer.

So you find out,
Without getting me riled,
Of what life's really like,

Potential anger sources all filed.

And don't start to think,
If I don't live with them,
That I can't be aboard,
From them I'll always stem.

So to get me off,
You have to help me see,
How things have been learned,
The power of the family tree.

And show me alternatives,
Ways to meet my needs,
Cos I won't get off this train,
Until I've new behavioural creeds;

New forms of transport,
To get me where I need to go,
Quicker, more effective
Not leaving me hollow.

And always remember,
You can't just give me a shove,
Cos I'll hold on ever tighter,

To the train, my anger, my love.

I have to open the door,
Alight on my own,
Be guided by your pointing,
My decision showing I've grown.

I can still love my family,
Accept who they be,
But choose my own transport,
And be the best version of me.

I SWORE

I swore, I swore with all my might that I would never be there again. I would never be that snivelling pile of patheticness. I would never mix snot and tears. I was done.

Done with feeling small, done with feeling useless. Done with being the butt of jokes, the butt of heels, the butt that you took yourself out on. Never, never again would I feel so low, so out of control, so at the mercy of another. Never, never, never.

Being in control became my mantra. Nobody was ever going to ride this horse. I was going to trot, to gallop, to canter through life and nobody was going to get in my way, nobody was going to make me deviate from my course. I was going to be in control now. Me and only me.

Little did I know what I was to become. The freedom that I thought I was creating for myself became my prison. I rose out of the ashes, I found a voice, I found some semblance of a self. Problem was that this self wasn't really me. It was a caricature of me, distorted by my desire to always be in control. I was to become that which I was running away from, a bully. It was my way or else.

The else showed up as aggression, passive or in your face. I would make people do what I wanted, or kill myself trying. I'd throw a tantrum, throw a chair, call you useless, swear till the air was blue. I'd make you feel weak, make you doubt yourself, make you dependent on me, be nice one minute and foul the next. I would stop at nothing in pursuit of my dream, of never losing control. I'd manipulate, I'd posture, I'd try and get my way. Control, control- my mantra.

And I lost sight. Lost sight of the fact that in my desire to be in control, I had lost control. Lost control of my life, of my direction, of my emotions. I was a slave to my anger, to my manipulation. I was blind to the fact that my dream of control was a nightmare. A nightmare for others and a nightmare for me; a toxic concoction of my past vulnerability. The stuff of life and relationships misconstrued, misunderstood and perpetuated again, ready to pour its poison into yet another life, into more relationships.

And then I met you. True to form I attempted to manipulate, to control, to dominate you. The world revolved around me; around my needs, my wants. I wasn't going to let anyone else cause me to lose control, least of all you.

So you'd try and get me to stop bugging that kid. Or try and teach me to compromise when I didn't get my own way. Try to get me to calm down, breathe deeply, count to ten, walk away. But you never addressed my need to be in control, the stranglehold I was in. So it didn't work.

I couldn't walk away, I couldn't calm down, I couldn't compromise, I couldn't do any of the things you showed me. Because if I did I would lose control, and I was never going to do that. I swore, I swore with all my might that I would never be there again. I was never going to let myself be weak again. So no matter what the consequences were I stayed in control and I carried on as before. As long as I stayed in control, I was alright. No-one could touch me then.

But you kept on banging on at me. Kept on trying to get me to change, kept on trying to take away my tried and trusted methods of staying in control. You were hell-bent on getting me to surrender the security of what I knew for the vulnerability of what I didn't. So you left me with two options...

...I threw the tantrum, I whipped out my anger and I thrashed you. Words and vitriol. Slammed doors, kicked tables. I showed you who was in charge.

... I whipped out my best suit of compliance, of lip-service, made you think you were changing me. Anything to get you off my back, anything to make you think you were in control of the situation, in control of me. What a mug. I sucked you in, good and proper. Thinking you were in control, little did you know.

But either way, it continued. Nothing really changed. Nothing had changed on the inside of me, so nothing was going to change on the outside either. Except maybe that you declared me a lost cause. You'd shown me all the tools I could possibly use to manage my anger, what else could you do? So you moved me on, shoved me somewhere else, to work with someone else. Or left me alone to continue afflicting myself and others with my ultimate weapon, my control.

I swore, I swore with all my might that I would never be there again... but I needed to be. *I needed to understand my own experience of vulnerability to understand how I was now making other people feel.* I needed to reconnect

27

with myself, to reconnect with them; linking my pain with theirs. I needed to be taken to a place where I would swear, swear with all my might that I would never make anyone feel like I once felt. I needed to understand that the way to defeat my victimiser(s) was not to become one myself.

I needed to understand how and why I was trying to control everyone and everything and how it was not working for me. How my life was built on fear, not freedom.

I needed to understand that life is not rigid, that it necessarily requires some give and take, some flexibility in order to work. I needed to learn that control is not the be-all and end-all. That new and great things often emerge when an unplanned path is taken, that by allowing spontaneity into my life, I could spontaneously bump into some good stuff.

I needed to learn to communicate rather than trying to second-guess others. I needed to learn to resist the urge to try and control a situation by convincing myself that I knew what they were thinking, that I knew what they were going to do and acting on that. I needed to stop viewing things from my perspective and try and understand it from theirs.

I needed to realise that most other people were not operating in the same way I do, weren't held captive by control and weren't always trying to control me. I didn't need to constantly be afraid that the other person was trying to get 'one over' on me. I needed to grasp that interactions are in the main not about a battle for control, of manipulation, of domination- they are an equal interaction, free-flowing explorations of ideas, views, information, give and take. That in this climate of communication, where no one person's agenda trumps another that compromise is possible, and that there is no shame in conceding a point, having your mind changed by another. I needed to learn that this does not make me weak, but makes me ever so strong as I am learning, growing as a person, constantly trying to be the best I can be.

I needed to see that my view of others was often what led to an interaction turning into adversarial conflict. Because I thought everyone was out to get me, I would interpret everything they said and did as an attack, as them trying to control me, even when they weren't. I would attack back and try to control the situation, try and make it work out my way, and they would end up having to defend themselves. It would then be all their fault and nothing to do with my original perception and subsequent actions; I absolved myself of any responsibility. I needed to learn to be less afraid, less fearful of others, to see that I didn't need to control them in order to feel safe. That in trying to control them and our interactions I actually made things less safe. I needed to trust and to hope in people more.

I needed to learn to open myself up to the possibility of something good rather than the expectation of something bad. In expecting the worst of people I limited the possible outcomes. Negativity and hostility breed negativity and hostility. I needed to realise that if I approached life more positively with higher expectations of others, with a more positive view of their motives then a good response is more likely in return and conflict lessens. Doing this is always a risk, and when fingers have been badly burned already, this can seem like an impossible task. But I needed to appreciate that even when positive expectations are not met and I am met with negativity, then I at least know that it is them with the problem and not me. I get to dust myself off and move on. I can't control them, they can't control me. Whichever way I look at it, freedom results; I'm not trapped in my own negative cyclone of control.

And once I learned all this, then I needed the tools- the calming techniques, the counting-to-ten, the walking away, the positive self-talk. The tools to give me the space to unlearn my negative learned behaviours. The tools to resist the urge to continue as before, to erupt, to manipulate, to control. The tools to allow me to rise above the moment and see the bigger picture. The tools that afford me the opportunity to choose me and a life of real control; of self-control borne of a better understanding of myself, rather than a life dictated to me by a fearful control that only ever brought less control, not more. I needed to see the point of the tools and how they related to me, what thought processes and ingrained responses they were trying to override before they were of any interest to me. Understanding my pact with the control devil always needed to come first.

I swore, I swore with all my might that I would never be there again. Until you understand this and I understand this, the control devil will always win and no tools you try and use to fight it can even scratch the surface of its skin. Exposing the control devil for what it is always leads to its demise and the tools keep it down there, keep it down out of the way. Down beneath my feet where it belongs.

-
WHAT TO DO?
-

IN THE HEAT:
PERFORMANCE OR RAGE?

One of the first steps in effectively dealing with anger in a teen is knowing what you are really dealing with, and this will vary from person to person, from situation to situation. At its very base level it is all about 'reading' their anger and establishing what they are trying to achieve by being angry and assessing the level of control of their actions. It is only by taking this step that we can appropriately deal with the angry teen in front of us.

PERFORMANCE OR RAGE?

The core distinction is between a controlled performance and out-of-control rage. Often 'anger' is merely a 'baring of teeth' performance like when you initially step into a dog's territory. The teen is very much in control of what they are doing and in essence they are trying to manipulate you or a situation with their anger. They may experience a physical feeling of anger so it isn't completely fake, but it is something they control. Their anger is a means to an end, with the end being making you go away, or making you chuck them out of class, for example. With out-of-control rage, however, there is a sense that they are a savage dog that really could bite, although they might not. You just don't know what's going to happen next, and that's a bit scary.

One of the easiest ways to tell the difference is in how the teen is physically responding to their anger. If they are showing signs of physical agitation like sweating, going red in the face, not being able to stand still, pacing, shaking, crying, clenching their jaw or fists or breathing quickly then it is highly likely that they are at least entering the rage danger zone.

If they are just being verbally abusive or are getting physical with other people or other objects without demonstrating any of the above traits, it is likely that they are just manipulating the situation to try and get their own way. It's more bluff and bluster than a raging bull.

You might not always be able to immediately tell whether you have a performance or a brewing rage in front of you, particularly with first anger encounters. Many performances are extraordinarily convincing, even to the point where the teen themselves has managed to convince themselves that they are in fact in a rage. However after a few incidents you can usually tell, either because a performance loses its convincingness after the first few shows, or because it becomes clear that they suddenly simmer down after they get what they want and there are no physical hangovers from the outburst, such as continuing to be red in the face or out of breath. It is like a switch being flipped, and that is because they have chosen to flip the switch.

More often than not, the anger you see will be primarily about manipulation and will be a performance. Rage is also a form of manipulation and it often appears when other forms of manipulation have failed. The young person descends into a blind panic and will do anything to get what they want. However, at the point when the 'fight or flight' response kicks in, the adrenaline surge occurs and they can't think straight, the manipulation ceases to be controlled and enters out-of-control rage territory.

It is vital that you can tell the difference between these two sorts of anger as your approach to each will vary massively. You will be better able to target your response in the midst of it all, later in terms of sanctions, and in the long-term in how you ultimately try to help them address their underlying anger issues. Use the wrong approach for the wrong type of anger and you will likely get absolutely nowhere.

It is not only the young person that benefits if you read their anger accurately either. A personal benefit for you is that you better preserve your emotions and your sanity. You don't end up feeling and exhibiting a danger response when it is only a performance. When you see the manipulation for what it is, it is far easier to stay perfectly calm and respond in a measured way, benefiting them and you.

MISREADING ANGER: A CASE IN POINT

One classic example of misread and misunderstood anger that led to inappropriate sanctions within my workplace involved a lad who repeatedly told workers to 'fuck off', no matter what they were talking about. They were incensed, told him this was outrageous behaviour, reported him to their managers (and to the courts on a couple of occasions), 'I'm not tolerating this angry rude boy' and he was moved onto someone else's caseload.

Then his file landed on my desk. And surprise, surprise, when I met with him, he repeatedly told me to 'fuck off' through our first session, then the second, and so it went on until about the fifth session. It was unpleasant, but he wasn't in my face with it, and it was obviously a fairly benign strategy to make me go away. So I ignored it and eventually he stopped. He then even started to engage with me and we did some great work that led to significant change in his life.

The problem was that he had used his swearing strategy with so many workers before me and with great success. They had responded in exactly the way he wanted them to. His swearing was a calculated strategy that worked a treat for him and protected him from the vulnerability of addressing his real anger issue- that he had repeatedly experienced violence at the hands of the men in his life. So for him, being allocated yet another worker wasn't a sanction, it was a present.

Furthermore, by workers repeatedly not 'reading' his anger correctly and employing the wrong sanction, his negative and confused view of workers and adults in general was confirmed. On a very deep level his confusion about attachment was reinforced. He needed and deep-down wanted attachment, but he was scared of the reaction to 'putting himself out there', of being rejected again. So he threw up a smokescreen of anger to divert people from his real issue and to make them go away, which only reinforced his idea that workers didn't really give a damn about him because they ended up dumping him. His self-fulfilling prophecy worked brilliantly.

So going for a heavy-handed, 'I'll report you' approach was completely counterproductive. It didn't help him one jot and gave him exactly what he wanted. Perseverance and a gently-gently approach was required while he tested me out. On the sixth time of meeting with him he clearly decided I wasn't so bad and we took the first steps to really interacting and getting to the root of his real anger.

That couldn't have happened however, without that initial step of reading his anger and establishing what he was trying to achieve with it.

Obviously ignoring a behaviour isn't always the best strategy. With the swearing lad, ignoring him was the most powerful and appropriate sanction in that situation. His sanction from me (which ultimately led to a real reward) was that he didn't get what he wanted.

Sometimes it feels like we need to be seen to be doing something to deal with inappropriate behaviour. Actually it is often doing nothing (on the surface anyway) that garners the best results. Being 'all over a kid' for performance behaviour is often the biggest reward we can give them and only encourages them to continue down the same road.

RESPONDING TO MANIPULATION

I appreciate that the ignoring approach is easier to adopt in a one-on-one situation (although there are clearly limits as to what you can ignore) and is much harder to apply in a group setting like a classroom or youth club. We want to send out a consistent behaviour message to all of the kids, so nipping poor behaviour in the bud is important, and consequently ignoring isn't always an option.

In this context we need to consider what they are trying to achieve with their behaviour. Are they just trying to wind you up because they're bored? Do they want to be thrown out the class so they can meet up with some mates they've seen out the window? Are they stressing out that you've just suggested an activity that they think they are hopeless at and they don't want to be embarrassed in front of their mates? Are they finding the work too hard and want to avoid having to do it? What's their game?

Once you work this out, which will require some quick thinking, make sure you do not give them what they want. By all means, meet the underlying need if appropriate, like assisting them with the work that they are having difficulties with, or reassuring them that it doesn't matter if they are not brilliant at an activity and that there is pride to be had in trying, but do not meet the need in the way the teen is trying to get you to.

For example, if a teen does not want to participate in shooting some hoops in a youthwork or Physical Education session due to general low self-esteem and a belief that they are hopeless at basketball, they may well start acting up to try and disrupt the activity so they don't have to make a fool of themselves. Rather than focusing your attention on the misbehaviour, focus your attention on showing them that no-one is perfect, that you and their peers can miss shots too.

Injecting some humour into it can often work wonders. For example, calling each young person a famous basketballer and doing a running commentary along the lines of, 'Michael Jordan prepares to shoot... hear the crowd roar... and despite his valiant effort he misses. There's no keeping this guy down, he'll be back", gets the potential group disruptor interested or at least distracted from misbehaving, can massively reduce the pressure on them to 'perform' and makes it fun for everyone no matter their natural talent.

The end result is that their need to feel emotionally safe and free from an expectation of a perfect performance is met, not by opting out from engagement with the activity with poor behaviour, but by a demonstration from you and their peers that the activity is emotionally safe no matter how 'good' or 'bad' they are at the activity. Overall you make it clear that it is the process, the trying and the taking part, that is the achievement and the source of pride and praise, and not just the absolute end result.

If you meet the underlying need in the way that the teen desires, all that will be achieved is a reinforcement of their negative behaviour response. This is your opportunity to show them that there are more positive, constructive methods of meeting their needs and overcoming their fears than running away.

Sometimes, however, the manipulation is nothing more than an exertion of power and this is the underlying need they are trying to meet- the desire to feel in control of a situation, other people, and often you specifically. This could be due to having had experiences in life where they were controlled by others and they do not wish to feel so vulnerable again, or it could be something as simple as them being strong-willed characters.

Whatever the reasons, not giving them what they want is a far easier prospect on paper than in reality, particularly when precisely what they want is control. If their modus operandi is manipulation they are not going to be easily put off by a 'no', are they? Far more likely they will ratchet the whole performance up a notch, if not two. Furthermore, the more you assert yourself, the more likely it is that they could tip over from controlled manipulation into out-of-control rage. After all, in their minds, how dare you tell them what to do?

So how do you prevent them from inappropriately seizing control without ending up with an epic and escalating battle on your hands?

The best advice I have found on this subject comes from a leading expert on strong-willed children, Cynthia Tobias (2002). Her methods, work, they really do.

PROVIDE FIRE ESCAPES

From the earliest possible opportunity provide them with an opportunity to step back from the brink, to metaphorically escape through the fire escape from the situation they have created.

As Tobias highlights, the biggest tool you have in achieving this is humour. Her favourite phrase is 'Nice try', then smile and stop talking. One of two things will then happen, they will either back down or dig in their heels. "But you just gave him the opportunity to decide and to save face. Instead of going on the attack, which serves only to reinforce his resistance, you've taken down the first line of defence with the simple tactic of humour" (Tobias 2002:47). In doing this you are giving them the chance to make things right, to stop for a moment, to consider and possibly reconsider their position.

ASK MORE QUESTIONS

If you suspect they are kicking off for a particular reason, don't automatically assume that you are right. Don't start dealing with them accusatorially or confrontationally based on this assumption because, shock horror, you might be wrong. And if you are wrong and have responded inappropriately you will only succeed in turning a little fire into a full blown blaze.

I strongly believe that questions lie at the heart of good communication and good relationships. With well worded questions, communication then is about exchange, not assertion, enquiry rather than assumption, understanding rather than ignorance. Communication and relationships become more peaceful, constructive, more human. Good respectful questions have the power to reduce to a flicker even the strongest of anger pilot lights.

Good respectful questions aren't just in the words, they are also in the context. The best results occur when they are asked out of the glare of the group spotlight, just outside the room or in a quiet corner. Questions such as:

'Is there anything I can help you with?'

If there is an immediate tangible issue that they are trying to avoid, asking this question provides you with an opportunity to help them constructively face it and for you to help meet it. It shows a real desire on your part to understand which can only help to open rather than close the lines of communication.

'Are you trying to get in trouble, and if so, I'm really interested to know why?'

This question used in conjunction with a good sense of humour can resolve a situation in no time at all. If they were kicking off due to boredom, or just to wind you up for fun, or just for some attention, then asking them this question straight, with a smile on your face, can often lead to a little grin from them and an open confession. You can then look to try and re-engage them with the task at hand and give them some positive attention.

You can also provide them with some pointers, such as, 'If you want to get my attention just talk to me, right? If you start to muck around you're not going to get the best sort of attention from me, are you? Wouldn't you rather talk to me in a good mood, than all narky cos you're being a pest? We can make this work so much better. Just talk to me properly, and even if I can't talk to you or help you right there that moment, I will always try to find time.'

Not only will you have de-escalated the situation but you have shown them that you are interested in them.

Particularly needy children do demand more attention, and if they feel they aren't getting any they may resort to trying to get negative attention, as in their minds it's better than none at all. This can be particularly problematic in group settings where you have several, if not an entire class full of teenagers competing for your attention. You can easily resolve this issue by making it clear to them that they can get positive attention from you, if they ask for it at the right time and in the right way.

Set aside time for them, maybe at the end of every session and I promise you that that regular promise of positive attention will significantly lessen their need to get your negative attention through misbehaviour. They will probably become more focused on the tasks they have to complete also, be less easily distracted and less likely to become bored as they will increasingly wish to please you, as they wish to maintain a positive relationship with you. Remember that for many troubled teens, their relationship with you might be one of the only positive ones they have with an adult.

'Do you know why I asked you to do that?'

Strong-willed teens have very strong convictions and it is not enough for them to be told to do something just 'because I said so'. At the heart of this is a desire (usually at a subconscious level) to measure what they are being asked to do with their own convictions. They basically want to know what the big deal is.

By asking them you encourage them to consider this for themselves, and if they aren't sure you provide them with an opportunity to enquire further. You are "creating a dialogue in which mutual respect can flourish" (Tobias 2002:52).

So if you ask them why they think you are wanting everyone to play basketball, you assist them in considering that you are not asking to make them look stupid like they initially thought, but you are asking everyone so that you can build some team spirit and to help everyone to get to know each other. You help them to perceive things the way they were intended, not the way they interpreted them. This way, the task becomes less intimidating.

Or if you ask them why you asked them to quieten down in class, you assist them in thinking about others and not just themselves. They might have been being loud, acting the class clown to get their peers' attention, and when you asked them to be quiet they got annoyed because you were denying them the opportunity to have their need for attention met. However if you help them think that the reason why you were asking them to quieten down was because their peers could not concentrate on their work then they start to consider others' needs and not just their own. In essence, if they understand where you are coming from, then they are more likely to be led where you behaviourally want them to go.

So if their behaviour is meeting a need for them, be it attention, control, escape, avoidance of vulnerability, don't let them continue down this road and allow them to meet their need in this destructive way. This does not mean that you should ignore their need, but that you should endeavour to understand and better meet their need. Do this, and they will hopefully come to realise that there are better ways of having their needs met, that does less damage to others and less damage to themselves, and along the way helps them to build positive respectful relationships. This way you help to prevent an anger situation from growing from a few sparks into a raging fire.

However, sometimes due to deep emotional trauma or an inability to regulate their thoughts and emotions, either through lack of practice, lack of good role-modelling or physiological or developmental difficulties, manipulative behaviour can quickly become an out-of-control rage. Not getting their way, meeting their need in their usual angry way can cause them to panic and they unravel, losing control of themselves.

For some, manipulation was never a real feature of their behaviour and their anger response is a nought to sixty affair, a purely primitive, physiological, panicked, out of control response. Irrespective of whether manipulation featured first or not, a different approach is required when anger becomes rage.

RESPONDING TO RAGE

The beginnings of rage are usually identifiable when verbally expressed anger becomes physical- when violence is expressed towards another person, when the wall has to be punched, or when the signs of physical agitation as outlined at the beginning of this chapter, are shown (e.g. angry crying). It doesn't have to result in violence towards another, just in an outward physical manifestation. This is when you really start to wonder what they are going to do next. There is a sense that they might explode or even implode. This is the golden moment where reading the situation accurately and quickly will maximise the chances of being able to de-escalate their anger and to stay in control of the situation.

STAYING IN CONTROL

Your top priority at this point is to *de-escalate*. Even if the beginnings of their rage is as a result of you already discussing their behaviour, drop it. It can be picked up again later when they are calmer and you might approach it slightly differently in light of this response.

The keys to de-escalation are ensuring they have *physical space* and are at least a room away from whatever or whoever is stimulating their anger (this may well be you or another teen), you need to *stay calm yourself* and you need to give them *mental space* to calm down.

When people are panicking about what someone might do, they often talk more than they usually do, and this applies to professionals too. In this situation it is imperative that you *resist the urge to over-talk*. You'll only end up further over-stimulating an emotionally overstimulated person and it will only wind them up more. Don't choose that moment to tell them that their behaviour is unacceptable and to deliver your moral sermon. Don't deliver notice of your sanction either. You'll only be told where to go. There is plenty of time for that later. I have witnessed the catastrophic effects of such an approach, many a time. The results are not pretty- don't go there.

I have seen other practitioners do this. I have done it myself. The teen will do whatever they can to stop you talking, or to ensure they cannot hear you, in the quickest way possible. Making you stop talking often involves something being thrown at you. I have seen many fine aeronautic displays involving chairs, tables, staplers and even shoes.

Ensuring they cannot hear you often involves a swift exit. The biggest mistake I made one time was to over-talk while standing in the doorway of a room, because they were going to listen to me and what I had to say and I would be brave and stand my ground and make my point. All I succeeded in doing was driving the teen to new heights of uncontrolled rage and I paid the price of being shoved out of the way against a wall as they departed. In discussion with the teen a week later, my deepest suspicions were confirmed; he was not listening to a word of what I said. He was deep in the throes of his rage and all my voice was to him was a noise like an alarm that he had to get away from. In his red haze and with his haste to leave, he was not even fully aware that he had shoved me aside.

Don't reflect their anger back at them. If they sense you are riled, then their anger will only feed off your anger and de-escalation becomes much, much harder. This is where saying less and keeping it very simple often helps. Also speaking in a relatively quiet voice rather than trying to shout over them encourages them to tone it down, rather than crank it up further to compete with your shouting. Yes you may well feel like shouting at them, but your top priority is to get them down from the peak of their anger and to give them the mental and physical space they need to calm down. Only once this occurs can any meaningful communication occur.

Give them the *barest and simplest of instructions*- "Go and wait outside please. I will come and speak to you in five minutes", for example. Don't enter into a debate with them or get distracted by them throwing out further abuse or cheek. Calmly repeat what you want them to do until they do it. They will soon realise you are not about to have an argument with them and that resistance is futile.

If they want to leave the building, let them. The alternative is a bop on the nose, a broken window, or a hole in a wall. I know which one I'd opt for every time. Yes, it would be better if they didn't walk out, but you can factor that into the sanctions equation when you deal with them later. Top priority is to keep yourselves and others safe, and them too. Letting them choose the 'flight' rather than 'fight' option is one way to do this.

THE SAFETY OF CONTROL

In tackling their rage in this way, you preserve your own dignity and save them from doing something that they could really regret. No serious damage is done and they will come to respect you at some level, for having retained control of the situation.

When children and teens are angry and it is allowed to spiral, they themselves feel very unsafe because they don't know what they are going to do next either. By staying in control of the situation and managing them effectively, they will begin to associate you with safety. This can only help them to feel safe enough to hopefully eventually share with you the deeply personal issues of their lives, and allow themselves to be emotionally vulnerable in your presence. Then you can get down to really helping them change their lives and their behaviour.

No anger intervention works unless the anger is read correctly and treated for what it is, controlled manipulation or out-of-control rage. You could deliver the most brilliant anger management interventions but if you apply the wrong sort of intervention or sanction to the wrong sort of anger, then I'm sorry, but you'll get nowhere. Understanding is key, both during an anger episode and afterwards. The understanding once the dust has settled, is to what we now turn.

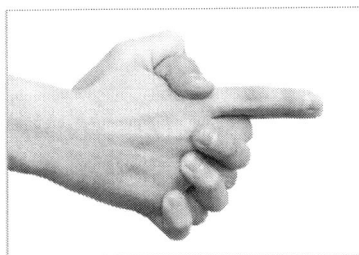

ANATOMY OF A TRIGGER:
THE ANGER DEBRIEF

Teens often don't know what they are doing or why they are doing it. They 'live in the now' in a way that adults often dream of. Yesterday was old news, tomorrow is a millennium away. They are also single-minded forces of nature. They are human juggernauts. They just plough on, full steam ahead.

All of this is what can make teenagers so resilient. Their interminable drive takes them places and even when they get knocked down, that momentum means they get right back up again. The problems come however, when they have taken a wrong-turn, like going down the pot-holed road of destructive anger. They often don't know how, or even have a desire to press the brake, look at a map and correct their direction. Instead they plough on ahead, going down a road full of potholes, somehow thinking that this route is just fine.

Even when they are lying in a pothole with their wheels in the air, they don't take the time to reassess their direction and they flip themselves over and carry on as before. Their ability to completely live in the moment can prevent them from properly assessing how today's pothole was the same as yesterday's and tomorrow's is likely to be the same. Even if they could do this their raging hormones and conflicting emotions damage their eye-sight so even though the holes are the same, they probably don't look that way. Their blurred vision also means that they have little realisation that every time they land in a pothole they take out passers-by. On and on they go. Is there no stopping them?

Well the good news is that you can stop them, or at least slow them down, pot-hole by pot-hole, but timing and technique is everything. It requires a commitment of time, of patience and learning. And your tool? The anger debrief.

THE ANGER DEBRIEF

In short, the anger debrief is when you sit down with a young person and go over what has happened in an anger incident to try and find ways to avoid it happening again. You are gathering information so that lessons can be learned– for you and for them. Depending on the complexity of the incident and the complexity of the teen this might take ten minutes or it might require a longer term commitment of time.

TIMING

Military debriefs happen after a mission has been completed. They do not happen when soldiers are firing off rounds. Same applies with anger incidents- it has to be over before you start. You don't walk into the middle of an active battlefield, people will get hurt. There is also too much noise, you won't be able to hear each other. So make sure that the battle is well and truly over. One night's sleep is the minimum I usually give it. The emotions will be less raw "cos yesterday was like a hundred years ago", right?

THE CORE PRINCIPLE: STOP & THINK

The baseline thing you are trying to achieve is to get them to stop moving for half a second and to get them to think. You might have to steal their wheels and they will certainly display their disgust (usually through the body language that screams 'get lost'), but it is vital that they think. Even if they scowl and pout through the entire process and say precious little (to save face), if you are talking about the right things, I can guarantee they will at least think. Reflection is a vital thinking and life skill and important to self-development and ultimately self-regulation.

SO WHAT TO TALK ABOUT? WELL REALLY, WHAT TO LISTEN ABOUT?

Make a point of emphasising that you are trying to understand what happened and are really interested in listening to them. You want to avoid this happening again and want to see what you can both do to help. This will prick their ears up if nothing else. Teens are used to you spouting, less so to you listening and talking about sorting the problem collaboratively. They are used to hearing 'you must do this', 'you must do that'. Start talking about 'we' and they will quickly get the idea that you are serious about helping them.

TRIGGERS

Once your desire to collaboratively work with them is established, the conversation can then move on to directly explore the sources of their anger, commonly referred to as their 'triggers'. Simply put, this involves asking them what was winding them up?

Giving them an opportunity to voice their grievance (even if it was unfounded) is the first step to them beginning to understand, express and regulate their emotions. Try to say as little as possible, and certainly at this point don't judge or criticise what they are saying, even if you strongly disagree. The fact that you have listened or are willing to listen even if they are not talking, counts for so much. You can then discuss with them in a very supportive manner how their behaviour affected others and how, if they really think that they have a genuine grievance that they can more appropriately address them. It's a simple formula really: if you listen to them, they are way more likely to listen to what you have to say in return.

In many cases, they will come to realise for themselves that their problem with so-and-so wasn't really that big after all and was actually because they were in a bad mood and that their reaction was totally over-the-top. Or they'll admit that they were being manipulative. Teenagers can be refreshingly honest if you give them the chance and don't force them into a defensive position.

So often if you make teenagers stop and think and let them voice their issues, they give themselves the best therapy. Don't be tempted to talk too much at first or to give them a lecture because you can prevent them from learning and practising the art of self-talk as a way of thinking through and managing their emotions.

I know some professionals who try to avoid asking the 'what's winding you up?' question to the more emotionally volatile and aggressive teens because they believe that asking it will only cause them to fly-off-the-handle again- "It revisits the site of their anger". However, if you don't ever ask them what was winding them up, how can you possibly help them to deal with that issue in a more appropriate way? You'll only end up giving them generic and therefore not the best advice. You have to enter their world through enquiry if you are to ever begin to help them and when the stakes are even higher, the asking of the question is all the more important.

Whatever the level of volatility, just telling teens that their behaviour is unacceptable and going no deeper will achieve very little. While the outburst may have been unacceptable, the underlying reason may not have been. Remember they are allowed to feel angry, it's just what they do with it that can cause problems. You can't sweep anger under the rug with a quick 'it's unacceptable' approach. If you want to solve the negative manifestations of it, you have to talk about the roots of it.

Yes, talking about what gets them angry can cause them to begin to feel angry. However you can ease these feelings by reassuring them, 'I can see that this is making you feel angry and I'm only asking you about it so that we can find ways to help you cope with these feelings'. Sometimes the rawness of their emotions will then subside.

Other times they won't and sometimes you just have to 'run' with their emotions and give them permission to express their anger, 'Just let it out. Say what you want to say. You won't get into trouble. It will help me to understand'. They will probably start expressing things that you don't agree with, like how so-and-so is a total bitch and how she always picks on them and how that lad totally deserved to be punched etcetera, etcetera. Swearing will probably feature too. Just roll with it, don't criticise, don't comment. Just let them get it out.

Whether they can calmly talk about what sets them off, or whether you have to let them verbally vent, this whole process helps you help them in so many ways.

You have given them the opportunity to be heard and they will respect you immensely for it. They are then much more likely to open up to you which can only help them.

By listening you validate the anger emotion and clear up a big source of confusion for them- anger is not bad of itself, it is just when it is destructively expressed. Again, this increases their chances of openly and honestly talking with you as they need not feel shame about their anger.

By not passing judgement on their initial explanation of their anger outburst they will see that you really want to understand, which will motivate them to express themselves in the clearest possible way they can. The more they do this, the less they will come to rely on derogatory terms and language. I'm always amazed at how they self-regulate their language when they feel they are being listened to.

With clear expression their triggers will be more easily identified and you can work to avoid them being pulled, or in situations where they do get pulled, finding ways of helping them to cope and to regulate their behaviour.

TRIGGERS UNFOUND? LOOKING FOR POINTERS

Particularly with the more emotionally volatile ones, simply asking them about their triggers will probably not get you to the absolute root of their anger. Yet by letting them voice their surface grievances uninterrupted you can be on the receiving end of a whole list of potential pointers as to what the real underlying cause may be.

One girl I worked with was forever getting in trouble for being 'gobby' to members of the public, to the police, pretty much everyone, or so it seemed. But by letting her talk about how 'so-and-so really pissed her off' and how 'that copper deserved it', it soon became clear that she had a major problem with men. By letting her talk it was uncovered that even though on the face of it her anger outbursts were not gender-specific, they actually were. Hidden from open-view was the vital detail that prior to every incident there would be some form of what she perceived as a negative interaction with a man. This would stress her out, and she would then go somewhere and behave in a way that caused members of the public or police, male or female to verbally object to what she was doing, and then she would vent, uncontrollably.

After further exploring this hypothesis, it then came pouring out how she had been hit by her step-father for years and this was why she found any interactions with men a stressful experience. This then physically manifested itself with her kicking rubbish everywhere or doing some sort of criminal damage, which then caused passers-by or police to intervene and then she would verbally abuse them.

We were then able to work through her experiences surrounding her step-father and how that affected her interactions with men and how she could more appropriately deal with those feelings. After that point amazingly she didn't get in trouble again. It was like a switch being turned off in her head.

This was after five years of fruitless anger management programmes, where triggers were explored, but that never went beyond the surface triggers. Apparently she would always say that it was 'people telling her what to do' that made her angry, or 'people not minding their own business'. The person working with her would then effectively gag her and stop her from going any deeper by trying to address her surface triggers. She didn't feel inclined to go any deeper because she didn't feel very listened to and because the real issue was not being addressed, her behaviour didn't change. She spent many nights in police cells and very nearly ended up in a secure unit for it.

It is so important to realise that two line explanations of triggers will often not suffice, and particularly so for the most volatile and aggressive. You will need to commit to properly exploring those triggers in your debriefs to see what the real root cause is. If after your first debrief session you feel that there is more than a simple issue to address and that you cannot commit to a full exploration make sure they are referred on to someone who can. Just leaving it and hoping it will go away will not work.

MOVING ON

So once you have explored triggers or 'what winds them up' then you can work towards finding ways to avoid the triggers and/or find ways of expressing their anger more appropriately. It is only by listening first, that you will be able to provide the necessary personalised approach to practically addressing their anger issues.

Listening also enables you to make better-informed decisions about the most appropriate consequences to apply. While consequences are usually applied shortly after an outburst, often before the full debrief can take place, the fact that they are imposed after at least some sort of an enquiry on our parts helps to validate them in the eyes of the teen, particularly when our rationale for applying them is clearly explained (more on this in the next chapter).

As I have already said, a one-size-fits-all approach to anger management rarely works. I think this is largely because such an approach doesn't involve listening to them enough which is what they crave. That, and to be understood by others and to understand themselves. And to achieve this they need to overcome their teenage urge to carry on regardless and be given the time to stop and think. Just stopping them and quickly dishing out a general sanction will not work without the listening element on your part and the thinking on theirs. To this end the anger debrief is a must.

THE ANGER BALANCING ACT:
CONSEQUENCES VS RELATIONSHIP?

Once the 'bomb' of an anger outburst has hit, whether a controlled performance or an out-of-control rage, our attention inevitably turns to considering what our response to such behaviour will be. In some environments such as schools there are clearly defined disciplinary responses to certain actions and in others a greater level of discretion is afforded. However, in either environment the underlying questions, the underlying niggling doubts will often surface.

Can we navigate a safe road between sending a clear message that destructive anger outbursts are unacceptable and preserving a good working relationship with young people so that we can still work effectively and make progress? Will the imposition of a sanction, of some sort of penalty, undermine our ability to actually help a young person change their behaviour? Can we show them that there are rules to this thing called life and consequences if we do not comply, and yet still be sensitive to their individual circumstances? Can we impose sanctions, and not wreck the relationship? Surely it's one or the other but not both? If we dish out sanctions they're going to get the 'hump' and disengage aren't they?

Well not necessarily. It is true that anger outbursts mishandled by professionals often lead to the further disengagement of young people, making them angrier and less likely to make the necessary positive changes in their lives. They often end up feeling that they haven't been listened to, that no-one cares and that they have been rejected (again). They go right back to the beginning of their recovery process, if not further back than that.

However, as we will see, if we apply appropriate consequences and explain the rationale for applying them then the relationship and progress may not only survive but even thrive. Through careful handling, they can come to realise that we reject their behaviour and not them and that their behaviour and subsequent consequences imposed do not have to result in an irreparably damaged relationship. Consequences and relationships can be balanced and balanced well.

A WORD ON CONSEQUENCES, SANCTIONS & DISCIPLINE

When talking about consequences for negative behaviours, different terms are used. Some say 'consequences', others 'sanctions' and others refer to them under the broad umbrella of 'discipline'.

These words, and particularly 'sanctions' and 'discipline' are heavy with emotion and open to wide interpretation, often on the basis of our personal experiences with other people who have used those terms. 'Sanctions' and 'discipline' are often imbued with the image of a Sergeant-Major or a terrifying, emotionally cold teacher wielding a stick. Care, compassion and measured control often do not figure in the mental images that people associate with these words, and they therefore do not want to use these terms. They will often refer to consequences instead. Others do not have a problem with these terms at all.

In this chapter I use them interchangeably as the idea of each is broadly the same; that an inappropriate action is met with some form of penalty. The Oxford English Dictionary has the following definitions:

Sanction: threatened penalty for disobeying a law or rule.

Discipline: the practice of training people to obey rules or a code of behaviour, using punishment to correct disobedience.

Consequence: a result or effect, typically one that is unwelcome or unpleasant.

These terms can be used with the underlying notions of castigation, of blind application with the sole purpose of inflicting pain and suffering on the recipient. They can also be used with an undercurrent of intelligent and sensitive application, used within the context of an unconditional caring relationship to encourage a positive change in behaviour. Where they are used in this book, the latter should always be implied.

THE IMPORTANCE OF CONSEQUENCES

From the start, let's be clear- sanctions for inappropriate behaviour are very important. They are a part of life for everyone, so to let a young person get away with poor behaviour, even if there are huge mitigating factors, isn't actually doing them a favour. They need to learn to live in a school, a home and ultimately a society where behaviour deemed socially unacceptable incurs social sanctions such as the restriction of freedom in the form of a detention, a grounding, or a prison term. You might not necessarily agree with some of the social sanctions applied, but the reality is that they exist. We have to learn to live with those restrictions, and so do they.

While it may be tempting to go 'soft' with them on the basis of their troubled life and/or in order to preserve your relationship with them, it really is not going to help them. Teens need clear, consistent boundaries and if you don't give them that, then they won't know where they stand with you and this will unsettle them. This will limit their ability to feel secure in your presence and consequently their ability to allow you 'in' to help them.

If you are consistent but consistently 'soft' with them then they are bound to 'play you' and they will not respect you for it. End result is that they won't listen to what you have to say. Do you listen to the advice of someone you don't respect? I know I don't. What you'll get is lip service and no more.

When the temptation is to bend the rules due to mitigating factors, you need to consider what the consequences were for everyone else. If in a group setting, how did their outburst affect others? How did it affect you? In the interests of fairness to all parties involved, directly or indirectly, even if there are mitigating factors, they need to be treated in the same way. Explain this to them, supportively. Let them know why it is important that you treat everyone fairly and while you understand the difficulties they face and you want to help them with this, the behaviour was still inappropriate and the sanction still needs to be applied. Any other response and you are basically telling them that it is okay to treat people badly if you have a good excuse.

The bottom line is that there is never an excuse for verbally or physically lashing out, in seeking to destroy and it is only in applying the necessary sanction, equally and to everyone that they will learn this valuable lesson. And in so doing, they learn by association that you are fair- a safe and valued characteristic in the eyes of any troubled teen.

So there is no point trying to preserve your relationship with a young person by bending the rules or being soft in your application of sanctions. Yes, you might get on well, but real positive change needs more than just 'nice' chats. It needs respect, it needs both parties to listen and it needs supportive challenge of inappropriate behaviour. Anything else and you are just enabling and indirectly collaborating in their behaviour. You may be well liked but change needs more than this.

HOW TO DELIVER RELATIONSHIP-MINDED CONSEQUENCES

Make it clear that you reject their behaviour, but not them

The most troubled teens often do not realise that they are more than their behaviour. They have never been valued for who they are, never been loved unconditionally. Instead they have been repeatedly told how useless and worthless they are, and every time they behave badly, their feelings of utter wretchedness are further reinforced. It can often get to the point where they purposely seek to reaffirm what others have said of them and what they feel of themselves- they look to behave badly. At least this response is something they are used to, it's predictable and consequently, perversely, safe.

When dealing with any teen's behaviour, whether they are well-adjusted or not, it is vital that we challenge their behaviour and not the very essence of them. In challenging their behaviour we have to leave them with something with which to rebuild- a faith in themselves, a belief that they can change, that they can do better next time, a hope for a better future. If we cut them down at the same time as their behaviour then we contribute to the hope crushing, to the further diminishing of their self-esteem and further limit the opportunities for them to decide to try and do better. If they can see no hope in themselves then as far as they are concerned there is no hope for change.

This is the fundamental difference between a sanction of care, of guidance, of hoped for renewal and change, and one dished out with cold-hearted retribution at its core. The purpose of the latter is to harm, to destroy rather than build up. It is about the immediate response and not the long term goal. It is about closing communication and understanding, of killing meaningful relationship rather than building it.

If you cannot see the positive purpose of a sanction, then you must question your motives. Even if you are not questioning your motives, the teen in front of you will be. The most troubled teens' default position is likely to be that you are just delivering a consequence because they deserve it, because they are rotten and bad.

It is vital that you check your motivation and if necessary change it. It is vital that they know that in delivering a consequence you are not rejecting them, but that you are trying to help them take responsibility, to choose a different way to behave that will help them be the best they can be. That ultimately you have faith in their ability to behave differently, that you believe they can shine.

Pace yourself & scale your sanctions

Don't go from zero to sixty miles an hour in no time at all. If you wheel out your biggest sanction first, then you have nowhere left to go. Obviously sometimes the first exhibited behaviour is so serious that it does warrant going to 60 immediately, but usually this is not the case.

The temptation to go to 60 in break-neck time even for a minor misdemeanour is that you will 'show them who's boss'. 'They won't mess with me'. This might work with your more well-adjusted teens, but your more emotionally vulnerable and volatile ones will not respond well. They will perceive you as unfair and will show you what they can do in break-neck time: blow up in your face.

Chances are they will have experienced someone significant in their life do this to them on a regular basis- going from 0 to 60 with no warning, often unfounded and often with emotional and/or physical damage to show for it at the end. In their eyes, you then become that person.

Immediately any respect for you goes out the window, any desire to co-operate with you, any ability to trust you and your judgement, let alone any advice you might offer. You make them feel unsafe and this will make them either fight or take flight. To undo this response will be hellishly difficult. It is better not to go there.

Yes, offer discipline and sanctions, but you have to do it fairly and in moderation. Troubled teens 'fairness radar' is finely honed. Life has often been very unfair to them so they will have a keen eye for it and won't co-operate if they detect it.

A far better approach is to have a scale of sanctions relating to the seriousness or the number of occurrences of the behaviour, that you are clear about in your head, and they are clear about in their heads. The benefits are that you are far more likely to be perceived as being reasonable and fair, not hot-headed. You will always get the 'oh, but that's unfair' knee-jerk response but an overall deeper view of you as fair is far more likely to prevail this way.

The relationship preservation credentials of this approach speak for themselves. If you're unfair you're a 'nob' or 'bitch' and not worth listening to, if you're fair then maybe there is something in what you have to say and they will keep on engaging, even after the sanction.

A scale of sanctions also has an important role in fostering a sense of responsibility, of self-control and choice in the minds of teens. If they don't know what your scale of sanctions is, then they don't know where their behaviour could lead them. You are consequently in charge of where their behaviour takes them. But it should be the case that they are in control of where their behaviour takes them. If they know in advance what the particular consequence will be of certain behaviours then you are putting the choice firmly in their hands. It's their choice and their responsibility as to how far they want to push it- they go into their behaviour with their eyes wide open. Just like we know that we will likely get a caution from the police for stealing a sweet, community service or a fine for persisting in this behaviour, and a definite prison sentence if we rob the sweet shop with a sawn-off shotgun- they should know the scales too.

As a result, it is then much easier to deliver sanctions later on in the process as they should know what is coming. Then they can never accuse you of not being clear with them, of shifting the boundaries or 'oh I wouldn't have done that if I'd known' excuses. The responsibility for their behaviour and the consequences is then firmly at their feet.

Surprisingly enough, this often productively feeds what some teens actually crave, some control and this is one area where we can gladly give it to them. Teens respond better to having the control and responsibility laid at their feet than they do to being dictated to.

Knowing the scale in advance also helps them to make an

informed decision when they are on the anger cliff-deciding whether to jump or not. If they know what t likely consequence of blowing up is, then they will be better motivated to try and exercise self-control, particularly when the consequence would incur a cost that they care about.

The upshot of responsibility being placed at their feet is that your sanctions then become less personal, and potentially less damaging to your relationship with them. You are just moving along a scale. The sanction then is about the scale, not directly about their relationship with you and your relationship with them.

Endeavour to make the consequences as personally relevant as possible

Blindly applying sanctions without thought for what the lesson is, beyond, 'they must do as I say' will likely not have any real impact on the teen. Consequences, on the other hand, that have been carefully considered and have direct relevance to the teen and their behaviour are far more likely to be remembered and to positively affect behaviour.

For example, getting a teen to spend their detention putting up posters where they have destroyed a display, or taping back together other students' posterwork, helps them to really see the damage they have done. This also provides an opportunity to ask them why they think you have asked them to do this, also demonstrating that you are not just mindlessly disciplining them, making you appear more fair.

Relevant consequences, such as this, also help them to understand the harm caused and can bring consideration of the victim(s) into their thoughts.

ions, including schools, make excellent use ative justice conference as a means of ictims of an incident. It is a tool that allows ave been most affected by an incident, perpetrator(s), to come together to share then ___ ___ , describe how they have been affected and develop a plan to repair the harm done and prevent recurrence, and thereby find a positive way forward.

Invariably sitting down and discussing these issues face to face enables the person who has caused harm to far better see the impact of their actions. Often a part of this process is agreeing with the victim how to repair the harm, and this forms the consequence. They are often very willing to participate and to be given the opportunity to a make amends once they have seen and understood the harm caused.

For many, they have never been allowed to even try to fix a behavioural situation, either at home or in an institutional environment and instead are just told to go away, or harshly punished, all for what they see as their core badness. If they are given the opportunity to fix a situation it inevitably demonstrates that you understand that while their behaviour may not always be desirable, you do not reject them and you believe in their capacity to change, to do it right- there is goodness at their core.

As a result finding the right consequence and delivering it in this way can be amazingly liberating, not only for the victim but for the perpetrator too. The consequence is therefore of utmost relevance to them and clearly has at its heart a desire to help the perpetrator, not harm them. (For more on restorative justice conferencing see the chapter, 'Why Don't They Care? Unveiling the Victims, Discovering Empathy' & *www.teenagewhisperer.co.uk/teenanger*).

Even when operating within a general scale of sanctions or consequences, as is often the case within an organisational setting such as education, youth justice or social care, there is usually some scope for personalising the consequences within the scale.

For example, a detention as illustrated above can be personalised, as can the sentencing within youth court due to the production of a pre-sentence report by youth justice professionals. Sanctions scales should not be so overly prescriptive that they prevent those operating within them from being able to use their professional opinion and their knowledge of the particular needs and challenges of a young person to respond within that scale, appropriately to the individual.

When using a referral sanction, remember you still have work to do.

Sometimes, however, behaviour escalates to such a point that a teen needs to be referred to someone with more authority so they can decide how to proceed. In these cases they may need to be referred to senior management, the police or the courts. However when doing this you must remember that you still have some vital work to do if you and the angry young person before you are not to take very many steps backwards in your relationship and your endeavours to help them.

Make it clear to them that their behaviour has left you with no choice.

Make it clear that you would do this with anyone and that you are not singling them out. This is particularly important as their skewed paranoid view of the world will probably lead them to think that they are being unfairly treated and you are making too big a deal of the situation. Your sanctions scale will greatly assist in this.

Make it clear that you are interested in hearing why they felt they had to kick-off.

Explain that the outward behaviour needs to be dealt with by someone more senior, or by the police, or the court if they are now in breach of an order, but that you are still interested in helping them to get to grips with their anger. All is not lost.

Make it clear that you are disappointed within the context of progress made, but all progress is not ruined. Keep looking forward.

Teens are very 'all or nothing', and the same applies to how they judge themselves. If they slip up slightly, they think that everything is ruined. This can really hinder them from continuing to make progress. They experience deep shame and a sense of uselessness and will disengage. Their anger at themselves adds to their anger pot, which will soon bubble over again.

The frustrating thing is that often everything is ruined when they slip up, but only because they thought it was and disengaged, rather than because it really was. This is yet another classic teen self-fulfilling prophecy.

So it is very important to keep them motivated to change and to see that they can still move forward. Often keeping the motivation alive can be achieved by exploring with them how their behaviour made them feel and how it made you (or any other victims) feel. By highlighting how the experience was a negative one for all concerned, you can then recommit to helping them address their issues. You can then explain to them how everything is not ruined, and that you can continue to make progress.

Clearly the reality sometimes is that no progress will have been made prior to the outburst. In this case your emphasis should be on exploring with them how their outburst made all concerned feel as a way to try and get them to the mental place where they will contemplate trying to change their behaviour.

Cultivating a sense of 'all is not lost' is obviously much easier to demonstrate when your working relationship with them will continue after the incident. However when a sanction involves a permanent exclusion from school say, or a custodial sentence where you will no longer be the allocated youth justice worker or social worker, then the relationship is most likely over.

However, if you have previously made progress with them, then explain to them that although you will not be able to work with them again, that they have made progress and that they can continue this, even if you are not there. Explain that efforts will be made to find someone to further support them in this but they are the captain of their ship, always have been and always will be. Anyone working with them is there as an assistant navigator and the direction they steer their ship is up to them.

Due to any attachment difficulties it is important that they also realise that they have not been rejected, but that their behaviour makes it impossible for them to stay. They can still make progress.

This is where the role of a mentor external to your organisation can be so vital. Your teen can hopefully form an attachment with someone who is not tied to a school, a youth club etc. This means that if they have to leave your organisation that they are not completely cast adrift, as it often seems to them, as they will have their mentor who will follow them wherever they go in life. So if you have a young person who is sailing close to the 'forced departure wind' try and find a mentor before and not afterwards. This way the damage of the exclusion to the young person's progress will be significantly reduced.

RESPONDING WITH DIGNITY

By choosing and delivering sanctions appropriately and openly with teens and seeking to help them understand the process and why you have to use them, any potentially negative relationship effects of sanctions can be minimised. Yes, they may go off in a 'huff' but if you give them time and if they have the opportunity they will likely eventually return. Even if they do not physically return, it is still likely that they will take a great deal from the sanctions process if delivered well and will reflect on it in the future.

Why? Because although they didn't treat you fairly and well when they got angry, you treated them fairly and well. Although they didn't communicate with you and others well when they got angry, you communicated well with them. Although they didn't stick to the rules and the 'system' when they got angry and they made everything unpredictable, you stuck to the sanction scale and the system and made everything predictable. Although they got behaviourally lost, you were still there as their signpost. Although they chose to make the wrong choice, you always chose to help them make the right choice. Although they tried to reject you with their behaviour, you didn't reject them, even if they did have to leave. Although they thought all hope was lost and everything was ruined, you showed them hope and how to rebuild.

You were the adult in all this. You gave them the stability, the security, the clarity and the guidance that they needed. And you showed them all this, not only in the good times, but in the bad, when you needed to dish up sanctions.

We therefore should not overly worry about sanctions damaging working relationships. Sanctions well applied with a heart of care can show young people how to live within limitations, to behave honourably, fairly and to have hope for positive change. It shows them how to have a relationship of respect based on measured calm actions rather than hot-headed knee-jerk angry reactions. We should not underestimate the lesson for them in how sanctions are delivered and that sometimes this is the larger message than what the sanction actually is.

WHAT DID I DO?
THE ANGER DEBRIEF FOR WORKERS

In every situation, good or bad, there is always something to be learned. Whether it is a 'yes, I really got that right', to an 'oops, I really screwed up there, must have a rethink' or somewhere in-between, progress will only be made if we open ourselves up to critical reflection and constantly try to improve.

This is often the fundamental barrier that we try to help young people overcome. Often they do 'screw up', problem is their solution is often to bury their heads in the sand and continue to make the same decisions and act in the same way. What they need to do is take the time to honestly reflect on their decisions and actions and to assess whether there is a better way.

Nobody likes to look in a mirror and face the possibility of having to reflect on how they've messed up. It requires honesty, a desire to improve and a willingness to accept and embrace personal vulnerability so progress can be made. This applies to teens. This applies to us as their workers or their parents. We can't expect them to do what we ourselves are not prepared to do.

So if we expect and desire teens to debrief their anger episodes, we should also be willing to submit ourselves to the same process. In essence this involves asking what our role was in their anger outburst (or series of outbursts), or more simply put, 'What did I do?'

By turning our attention to trying to answer this question we can take the positives, the 'what worked' and add it to our permanent toolkit. We can also pick apart the 'what didn't work', assess why and decide whether it is a strategy that needs to be resigned to a great big hole in the ground never to see the light of day again, or whether it needs to be used more carefully, in the right situation with the right person. We can then consider more appropriate strategies for a particular teen and good strategies in general.

In doing this we can only get better at what we do. Our work evolves, it becomes a refined, sensitive, responsive, informed engagement with teens rather than a generalised, clumsy, all-power-to-me and none-to-you disengaging process.

WHAT WAS MY ROLE IN IT? WHAT DID I DO?

So what do I mean by 'your role in it?'. Well it can be broken down into a number of questions:

DID I ENCOURAGE IT?

This particularly applies when talking about manipulative anger or anger that is purely a performance to get you or others to comply with their wishes (see chapter, 'In the Heat: Performance or Rage?', for the difference).

Teens are strategically shrewd beings. If they see a strategy that works, they will use it whenever they can (even when they don't particularly need to). So if you are going round and round in the same behavioural dance with a teen it is really important to stop and ask yourself if you are perpetuating it as much as they are. Do you always accede to their demands and on their terms? These demands may not be verbally expressed but that is what they are essentially demanding with their behaviour.

For example, picking a fight with someone in the group for saying something, not because they really care what was said but because they are manipulating the situation to get some attention from you. After all, negative attention is better than no attention. If you give them no attention beyond telling them off for their poor behaviour, sending them out etc. then all you are doing is meeting their need on their terms. Why on earth would they stop?

Instead, make the time and effort to meet their need in a more constructive way like giving them unsolicited positive attention so they learn that they don't need to create a situation to get your attention.

Meet the need but don't reward the negative behaviour or you'll see a lot more of it. Also be aware that they may meet their underlying need in a variety of ways- they may have a whole repertoire of strategies. So just because they don't use the same strategy each time you still need to question whether it is all essentially coming from the same 'need toolbag' and are you encouraging them to get their old trusted tools out instead of giving them some nice new ones?

AM I JUST APPLYING BANDAIDS?

If you never scrape below the surface of their behaviour and try to establish what underlying need they are trying to meet with it and help them to find appropriate alternatives (which could be achieved in your sessions with them or may require outside involvement) then you will probably not see the behaviour disappear. You can't apply bandaids to teenagers. They just won't stick.

So ask yourself, 'In dealing with this teen have I just been applying quick surface fixes?' They might solve the problem in the very short-term but will have no longevity. This is where the anger debrief for teens is so vital. It is your way of genuinely trying to help them by going deeper.

DO I HAVE A BIG HEAD?

You do not have all the answers. If you think you can fix all teenagers single-handedly then you are misguided. If you think you can just talk them all better then your chances of success immediately drop. Different teens have different needs and therefore require different methods of help.

After anger incidents you seriously have to ask, 'Is my strategy way off-the-mark?', 'Is it me that is getting in the way of progress?', 'Do I need to try something else?', 'Do I need to loosen my grip on the intervention?'

Also ask yourself 'Am I communicating my message to them in a way that they can grasp?' If their anger comes from a place of low self-esteem, talking about how to boost their self-esteem probably won't work and the anger outbursts will continue. Often trying to talk to them about what makes them feel like rubbish is precisely what will press their buttons. Getting them involved in something like volunteering that gives them that feeling of worth to other people and gets them thinking outside of themselves speaks way more than words. Their self-esteem will likely rise and their anger subside.

Are their anger eruptions as a result of high stress levels and no appropriate output? In which case putting them on spot all the time asking them about their feelings will probably push their stress levels into the danger zone and may cause an eruption. It might be that getting them involved in a sport to release tension, to channel their adrenaline into something positive may be the tool they need to help them control their emotions.

Whoever the teen, a whole package of measures usually works the best in my experience and often your role can end up being quite small in the general scheme of things. Don't think you have all the answers. Having as broad a range of strategies and tools at your disposal and learning from experience when and where to use them is all part of your anger debrief learning experience.

AM I DISENGAGED?

Teens have an astounding ability to make us feel totally useless. We try as hard as we can to help them, but they continue to play up. In these situations it is so easy to withdraw into our shells, tolerate their intolerable behaviour and never actually address the behaviour or the issues because no matter how we try we get nowhere. We declare that we just don't care anymore.

This is when we seriously have to consider whether we are disengaged and why. Have we withdrawn because we feel ashamed that we have not been able to help them, that they have somehow beaten us? And instead of doing what is best for us, and for the teen, which is to reach out to colleagues or experts and get advice and talk about various strategies to tackle their behaviour and needs, do we trudge on, going through the motions, sabotaging any hope of change?

The end result is that negative behaviours are reinforced

as they are not challenged. And from this place of shame, vengeful button-pushing can occur. Their anger makes us angry and into a downward spiral we descend. They sense we don't care, which only feeds their anger.

So you need to reflect and assess what buttons of yours they push. How do they make you feel? If you feel ashamed, why do they make you feel ashamed? Do you have personal issues that get in the way of you being able to help them? Are you obsessed with perfection or control? Does your inability to be the perfect worker or teacher and to be in complete control in this situation cause you to unravel internally? Is this why you just don't care anymore? Do they somehow sense this? Or is it just that they sense your lack of interest in them with their finely-honed radar and is this why they keep on kicking off?

This really requires soul-searching and a real hearty dose of honesty. Yet by searching our own selves we can also end up with the positive by-product of gaining insight into the teen's behaviour and having a new level of compassion and desire to help them.

DID I PUSH THEM OVER THE EDGE?

You will almost always play a part in them getting angry, even if it's just because you're wearing the same colour sweater as their Mum or Dad was when they had a big ding-dong with them that morning. But really, honestly, critically reflect on whether there is anything you can and should have done or not done to stop a situation from escalating from 'narkiness' and irritability to outright anger.

Do you take them to the point where their behaviour enters the unacceptability stratosphere? Yes it is they who are always ultimately responsible for their words and actions, but do you lead them there?

I say is there anything you 'can' and 'should' do because it is ever so important that you do not cave in to avoid an escalation. If you do then all that your teen will see is that by 'pretend' escalating that they will get exactly what they want. Your caving in will just reinforce this behaviour, not sort it.

What I am talking about is things that you say and do that can make things worse and unnecessarily push them over the edge. If you are staying calm and sticking to your 'message' and this winds them up purely because they disagree, then so be it. This will be a situation where they will learn that you have boundaries, you mean it, and you are not going to be moved, even by a force ten anger hurricane. You will then have to deal with the consequences and so will they.

Several classic unnecessary petrol bombs on the barbecue I have witnessed or committed myself are as follows:

WAS I 'IN THEIR FACE' LONGER THAN WAS NECESSARY TO GET MY POINT ACROSS?

Not backing off once you have delivered your message to give them time to process what you have said or done turns you into an insufferable nag who must be disposed of immediately, either by verbal or physical attack. To avoid this you need to give them thinking space and often actual physical space to calm down and take stock.

DID I HAMMER MY POINT HOME WITH A JACK-HAMMER?

Nobody likes being repeatedly told in a ten-minute period how their actions are unacceptable and even if you deep-down agree, the constant beration will cause you to flip. Everyone wants to maintain some sense of pride and dignity and a continuous assault will be counterproductive. Just as a jack-hammer will affect the structural integrity of concrete while a few little taps of a regular hammer will not, a tirade of disgust and disappointment will affect their core whereas a short, sharp and clear explication of the problem and why it is a problem will get through but won't do any long-term expensive damage. If nothing else, having you continuously jabber in their ear will overstimulate an already overstimulated person. Don't undo a good piece of intervention by overdoing it and causing them to erupt.

DID I USE ACCUSATORY COMMENTS OR PSEUDO-QUESTIONS?

Things like, 'What is wrong with you?', 'You need to grow up', 'Stop being so immature', 'Nobody else is behaving like this', 'Why is it always you?'.

Put yourself in their shoes. My buttons would be pressed if someone said that to me, even if there was an element of truth in it, and I'm pretty even-tempered. You are entering the territory of undermining them as a person, rather than seeking to address their behaviour. You are seeking to make them small and yourself big, a dynamic that doesn't get good results. There are far more diplomatic ways of addressing and exploring these issues, and not in the heat of the moment, but as part of your debrief with them later when everyone is calmer.

DID I PUBLICLY RIDICULE THEM OR EMBARRASS THEM?

Doing this is effectively an attack on their person and they will either take flight, or most likely if they have an outwardly expressed anger issue, fight. You should always try to avoid dealing with them publicly and definitely not in front of their peers.

Be careful not to use them as your behavioural show-pony to demonstrate to their peers how you will not tolerate such behaviour. This is an exploitation of the situation for your 'power' benefits. This is not about you, it is about them.

You can't socially ostracise or shame an often already socially ostracised and shame-filled young person into behaving. You will only push their buttons and make it ten times worse for them, and for you.

If you are in a group-setting, ask them to wait in the next room, in the corridor etc. This will hopefully give them time to calm down and will enable you to deal with them in a way that allows them to focus on themselves rather than their image management in front of their peers. They will then be much clearer that what you are saying to them is about resolution of a situation, not point-scoring.

In using this approach, there is also a clear consequence to their behaviour for the rest of the class to see. They can see that you are definitely in control and are dealing with the situation, respectfully and with dignity. If they behave similarly they can expect a similar response.

Honest self-reflection is way more likely if you respect their emotions, even if they have not respected yours or others. Do as you would be done-by. Would you appreciate a public dressing-down in front of your peers from your manager?

WAS I ANGRY WITH THEM? WAS I SUBCONSCIOUSLY SEEKING REVENGE?

Publicly ridiculing or comparing someone in front of their peers comes from a place of anger yourself. They've made you look or feel little so you respond in kind by trying to make them look even smaller than you. Put simply, it's revenge. It can also occur in a one-on-one setting. It can also occur without you even realising.

For example, do you ever find yourself bringing up one of their biggest issues in the midst of a tense could-tip-over-into-rage exchange?:

This could occur in public or private:

Kid comes into school / appointment late because the bus from their group care home which is on the other side of town was late again. Worker /teacher doesn't know this.

'You're late, AGAIN. What's the problem?'

[Grunt] 'I hate this bloody class/these appointments'

'Well we all have to do things we don't want to. You have to come so there is no point complaining.'

[Under the breath] 'Fat git / bitch'.

'I heard that. Don't think that just because you are going through a difficult time at the moment that you can talk to me like that'.

{Trigger pulled. Let the fireworks commence.}

I have heard far too many versions of the above conversation. Yes, it is true that there are boundaries for behaviour that exist independently of what may be going on in a young person's life and they do need to know this, but telling them in this way is not helpful.

As far as they are concerned you decided to hit them over the head with the awfulness of their life at a time when they are feeling emotionally vulnerable and insecure precisely because of the awfulness in their life. And what do we do when feeling vulnerable and pushed that little bit too far- we get as far away from that person as possible (flight) or we shut them up by other means (fight).

Yes, by all means acknowledge the difficulties in their life, but not at a point when there is a clear power or authority differential. Used in this way it becomes a weapon to make them feel small rather than an issue that needs to be compassionately acknowledged and addressed. You are deliberately trying to push their buttons (and often this is subconscious) in exactly the same way that they have pushed yours.

Revenge will ultimately get you nowhere. You will never be able to help them sort out their anger issues if they think that you are playing power games.

WAS I LISTENING?

When you see that a situation might escalate there is a massive tendency to internally panic as to where this could lead on the basis of previous performances and try to shut them down without actually listening to them. You try to nip it in the bud, but instead of gently using the fingertips, you get the chainsaw out and fell the entire bush. This is a sure-fire method to get mild annoyance to escalate to full rage.

Often the most effective way to nip it in the bud, is to actually allow the grievance to be voiced, acknowledge it and deal with it there and then if appropriate, or promise to deal with it later. Most of the time you don't actually really have to do anything other than just listen to them because once their annoyance is voiced, it leaves them and is no longer bubbling beneath the surface. Out in the open air it seems a lot smaller to them than how it feels when it is crammed inside them. Their anger loses its fizz.

A large part of managing an angry young person is in helping them to voice their feelings, so to try and shutdown them down when you see they are a little riled about something is the worst thing you can do. You can end up leading them to the anger place that you are so desperately trying to avoid.

WAS I CALM?

People reflect what is in front of them. That's why when young people are angry, you can so often get angry. And as they sense your anger, they get more angry. And it's not just about what you say, it's about what you do. So when debriefing an incident consider, 'What did I do with my body?', 'What did I do with my voice?', 'How did that affect what they did?'

If you get riled and start shouting or raising your voice, they will do the same. What you want them to do- do it yourself.

If you want them to stop shouting, talk quietly. If you want them to calm down, take a relaxed posture in your chair, even if it feels like the exact opposite of what you want to do and actually makes you feel quite vulnerable. Don't discuss an issue with you both standing because whoever is the taller will naturally feel more in control. Level the playing field and they will feel less under attack and so will you.

If you are standing, don't stand square on to them, stand slightly side-on, they will then perceive what you say and do less aggressively. Don't wag your fingers, don't put your hands on your hips.

Overall, be as physically passive as you can. In these conditions more measured emotions and communication will hopefully win the day.

GROWING IN HONESTY

So in trying to address anger issues in teens they have to be honest with themselves and so do we. Unless we constantly seek to identify and address any weaknesses in our work and celebrate and build on our successes then we are at best lazy and at worst damaging. Of course we won't always get it right and at times it feels like we are flying by the seat of our pants. But over time the good strategies and our ability to identify when to use them becomes more natural, more intuitive. The good work lays down roots and the not-so-good stuff rots down and fertilises. We just need to take the time to identify the difference. It helps us to grow, and helps the teens we work with to grow too.

WHY DON'T THEY CARE?
UNVEILING THE VICTIMS, DISCOVERING EMPATHY

When young people lash out at others, verbally or physically abuse them and cause them pain there is an automatic placing of personal need over that of others. Whether it is a need to vent, to express frustration, to divert attention, the feelings that trump all others are the feelings of the perpetrator. The person on the receiving end, be it a peer, an adult, anyone, is a victim of their emotional expression.

It is often the case, and particularly so with the most challenging of teens, that there is a seeming complete lack of care for the emotional and/or physical wellbeing of others. A large part of the issue is that they lack the ability and/or the desire to view their actions from the perspective of the people on the receiving end, to put themselves in their shoes. In criminal justice, this is often termed a lack of victim awareness, and in more general terms is often referred to as a lack of empathy- an understanding of another's situation, feelings, and motives.

With anger (and other teen behavioural issues), this is inextricably tied up with the issue that some teens have, of denying that there is even a problem. If they proclaim that they do not have anger issues then we can be sure that they are not fully seeing their victims, if at all.

They may in moments of quiet reflection concede that their behaviour does have some form of a negative impact on others, but we can be sure that they do not fully see the extent or depth of that impact, the amount of people affected and go as far as seeing them as victims of their behaviour.

If we want their behaviour to change, and if they are to see their behaviour as a problem and seek to change it, then they have to really *see their victims* and *understand their experience.*

However we can only successfully achieve this if we seek to *understand why they lack empathy in the first place.* For each teen there will be different combinations of reasons, some generally applicable to all teens and some only applicable to a minority. As we will later explore, our approach will need to be tailored to their particular combination of challenges.

THE RUNDOWN:
WHY TEENS CAN LACK EMPATHY

1.   Put simply, teens in general often do not reflect on how their actions affect them, let alone others. It's not a thought process that comes particularly naturally.

2.   Teens live very much in the moment, in the rush of their emotions, be it a buzz or a rage. They are so caught up with how they feel now that how others feel, then and

later, does not often enter their heads.

3. Even when most people would stop and reflect later, teens are often off doing their next thing, so don't allow themselves this time. This is why they can repeat the same damaging behaviour, for themselves and others. It just doesn't occur to them to do anything else.

4. Many teens do not know how they feel about a great deal of things, or how to express it. Consequently to ask them to put themselves in someone else's shoes can be a difficult ask.

5. Some teens' inability to accurately read body language, interpret facial expression and tone of voice means that they have little grasp of what other people feel, particularly when in a situation where they are caught up in their own emotion, or where their behaviour renders the victim speechless or submissive.

For some this inability is purely a result of the way that teenage brains function. Research has shown that teenagers brains function significantly differently from adults and they use different parts of the brain to identify emotions, and they often misinterpret.

In research conducted at the McLean Hospital in Massachusetts, teenagers and adults were shown pictures of adult faces and were asked to identify the emotion expressed (Yurgelun-Todd 2002). Using Magnetic Resonance Imaging (MRIs), researchers traced what part of the brain responded as subjects were asked to identify the emotion. The adults could correctly identify the emotion, whereas the teenagers could not. Moreover, the teens mostly used the amygdala , a small almond shaped region in the brain that guides instinctual or 'gut' reactions, while the adults relied on the frontal cortex, which governs reason and planning. As the teens got older, the centre of activity shifted more towards the frontal cortex and away from the cruder response of the amygdala.

It might also be that a teen is additionally unable to correctly interpret facial expression and body language because they have an autism spectrum disorder. This disorder makes reading these cues extremely difficult in the first place, and also makes socially imaginative work to try and put them in the shoes of another, very difficult. These difficulties are well expressed by Paul Siebenthal, an adult blogger with Aspergers:

"When I see a facial expression in isolation without context, words or prompts I get very little internal reaction. I am at best confused. I try and think my way around the situation looking at it in the same way as I would a puzzle. There is very little emotional response. In short I am lost. I struggle to know what I'm supposed to interpret from the expression. Sometimes even the words don't help. I am left with a blank space in my mind where I sense I should have some magic answer. I am told that when Neuro-typical people see expressions they read unconsciously the meaning of the expression. They get an emotional response and understanding of what is required by that person, at that time, based on that reaction." (Siebenthal: 2012)

6.   As for everyone, alcohol and drug use prevents the normal functioning of the brain. As a result, even the most caring person is capable of behaving in ways that are not the norm for them. Normal personality traits can disappear during intoxication and be replaced with selfish, angry and egotistical behaviour. Aggression and mood swings are very common as well as a general deterioration of morals.

Alcohol slows the brain's synapses and chemically alters the body by affecting serotonin levels, the chemical responsible for transmitting signals of mood in your brain.

These physical changes cause emotions to get out of control and cause adults and teens to do and say things they normally wouldn't do. It is therefore entirely possible that a young person's behaviour and associated lack of care is a chemically induced one, the effects of which can be significantly reduced by changing their drink or drug use habits.

For those who are dependent on substances, there are additional complications which predispose them to antisocial behaviour and an associated lack of empathy. Someone who is dependent on alcohol or drugs will become obsessed with their next drink or hit which will lead them to make decisions that negatively impact their own and others' lives. Furthermore in order to avoid having to address their behaviour and stop using they will constantly seek to minimise the effects of their actions. For those with addictions, specialist help needs to be sought.

7. For some teens, not caring about others is a basic dog-eat-dog survival instinct that they have had to adopt for themselves, or have learned from the significant adults in their lives.

When daily life is a real challenge, or perceived to be such, the tendency is to focus on the self and not be concerned with others. Resources must be gathered- food, money, and clothing - and reserves of things like emotional and physical energy must be maximised, to weather the 'winter'. Personal needs override the needs of others- it's a matter of survival.

However, the problem arises when this perfectly logical understandable drive to survive and of looking out for ourselves or 'our own' becomes a mindset and influences behaviour where an extreme self-preservation survival instinct is not required. It can lead to the internal justification of unjustifiable behaviour. For example, the mindset of, "We don't have much money for things, sometimes including food", leads to a justification for conducting street robberies (even when they do have enough money for basic necessities) because "I can't afford it".

8.   Teens (and adults too) like to believe things that will justify their behaviour and minimise, in their own minds, the effects on others. They will suck up any excuses they hear like a vacuum cleaner.

So they will latch onto things like it being okay to punch someone in the face because they deserved it, to rob someone because they've got it all and I've got nothing so I'm just redressing the balance, or that it's okay to spread a malicious rumour about someone or post a nasty comment on Facebook because it was only meant as a joke.

When we all do things that we know deep-down are wrong, there is an incredible urge to do something that will enable us to live with ourselves, to have internal peace. And due to the fact that there is usually a hell of a lot whirling around in the heads of teens, the sooner they can get rid of that uncomfortable feeling the better. The choice then is to 'fess up and face the wrong and endeavour not to do it again, or to bury the uncomfortable feeling with spurious justifications and minimisations of the behaviour- it wasn't so bad was it? Plus, it takes less time and requires less reflection to opt for justifying and minimising and we all know how fast teen life runs.

9.   When teens themselves have been on the receiving end of unjustifiable behaviour by loved ones, be it abuse or neglect, they seek to reconcile their love for that person with the unloving behaviour. As a result, they look for ways to justify others' bad treatment of them so that they can quell the internal emotional turmoil. An often unrecognised consequence of this, however, is that they

become well versed in justifying unjustifiable behaviour and start applying those excuses for their own behaviour towards others.

10. To teens, friends are the beginning, the middle and the end of everything. If their friends are also involved in negative behaviour, they will oil each other's excuse machines. Put a group of teens together and they could convince each other that cats bark. If enough of them say it and agree with it, it must be true, right?

11. With successful justifications and minimisations of the impact on others, behaviour becomes highly repeatable. If they personally gain something from their behaviour, be it materially, power, control or a buzz then they will look to be able to do it again and justifications and minimisations enable them to do this without a sense of guilt.

12. By avoiding the consideration of others' needs, they avoid having to take responsibility for their actions. By taking responsibility there is at least the tiniest possibility of having to change. When negative behaviours are actually a teen's coping mechanism, such as lashing out at others to keep them from discovering their internal pain, they will avoid having to make the change. Change is scary.

So they'll use their ignoring of the impact of their behaviour on others, or minimisations and justifications of their behaviour to shore up their coping strategy, come what may. They are also comfortable with their current approach, it is nice and predictable, so putting their need for some sort of stability will come before consideration of anyone else.

13. Some teens have learned not to care, and in the worst cases, have never learned to care. For the most disengaged, challenging teens, the paradox is that they

have often learned through experience that victims of antisocial behaviour don't really matter. And why? Because as a victim themselves, no-one cared about them. When they were victims of abuse or neglect, the perpetrator never cared about their needs, about their feelings. So why should they care about anyone else's needs? Rather than 'do as you would be done by', it's 'do as I was done by'.

So when they are acting out their unresolved, confused emotions, they genuinely don't care how they affect others. Their number one priority is often engaging in a behaviour that gets them what they want, or meets a deep-down unmet need.

They might be expressing their anger at a personal experience by lashing out at others, or expressing a desire to forget themselves for a while by getting a buzz from illicit substances and committing crime to feed the habit, or making themselves feel big for a moment rather than the usual smallness by robbing a school kid.

And this was exactly what was done to them. However they were used and or abused, was about their victimiser meeting their needs by using, abusing or neglecting them. At such a formative time, this lays down deep roots in their minds and can often end up with them acquiring the traits of their abuser because they don't know any different.

So there are a whole myriad of reasons why teens find it hard to consider the needs of others in addition to their own. Understanding that it often does not come particularly easily helps us, as workers or parents, to be more patient and understanding in addressing this issue and to take an individualised approach in helping them develop the vital social skill of empathy.

While any form of anti-social behaviour that results in

anyone being victimised cannot be excused with the reasons above, tackling the issue from a place of understanding will help teens to engage with us on the issue and to bring about the necessary change. We need to ensure we are not operating with an empathy deficit when dealing with theirs.

WALKING TOWARDS EMPATHY: IT'S ALL IN THE SHOES

So we know what some of the issues could be. We know with near certainty what some of the issues are. But what do we do? How do we get them to start covering the distance between their actions and the impact it has on others?

Irrespective of the particular reasons for a young person's lack of empathy, the following steps will at least start them on that journey.

During that journey our knowledge and our inklings regarding their particular empathy difficulties will cause us to focus on some areas for longer than others, be particularly sensitive on some painful pathways, and ensure they do not take a responsibility detour along the way. But they have to take this journey if their behaviour is to change and if they are to sustain that change.

And how do we get them to do this? The answers are all in the shoes.

SELF-CONNECTION:

HELP THEM TO WEAR THEIR OWN VICTIM SHOES

One of the keys to getting them to consider others feelings is to help them reflect on their own victim experiences first. This can seem massively counter-intuitive. You get them to think of others by getting them to think about themselves? Isn't their self-absorption the problem? Won't I just feed it?

When trying to change anything with a teen (or anyone for that matter) the best way in, in my experience, is to start from the exact point where they are at. What you say then becomes very relevant and very interesting to them, they feel a connection with you, that you 'get them'. Your potential to influence them consequently exponentially increases.

The idea is that if you get them to think about themselves, and to assess why they care about what other people do to them, they will begin to see that they need to care about what they do to others. Meet them where they are at, and you'll be better able to lead them to where you want them to be.

So if they are violent, get them to think about when someone was aggressive or violent to them. If they rob others, get them to think about when someone has taken something from them, or when they were scared, when they didn't know what was going to happen next. If they break things, punch holes in walls or smash windows when they are angry, get them to think about when something of theirs was broken. Their own victim experience doesn't have to be as serious as when they victimised someone, just a situation where similar feelings would be aroused.

In essence, the mental process you are teaching them is how to apply their own experiences to help them put themselves in the shoes of another person. And this has enormous preventative power.

Behaviour that victimises others usually comes from a place of extreme depersonalisation. The injured party (physically, emotionally or materially harmed) is turned into an inanimate object without feelings. This is particularly acute in the case of corporate victims (e.g. with vandalism when it is a bus company that has to repair a smashed-up bus shelter resulting from an angry teen and a crowbar). If you help them find points of connection between themselves and their victims (past or potential future) then their ability to minimise the effects of their actions is severely curtailed and they are way less likely to persist in their negative behaviour.

Engaging in this process will also help those who have been the victims of serious abuse and neglect themselves, work through their feelings that no-one cared about their feelings as a victim when they were being abused.

Where you know that abuse has taken place, it may be particularly useful to first talk in general terms about what it feels like to be a victim, without particular reference to their negative victimising behaviours. Show them that you care that they were a victim and that you are interested in what they have to say. Show them that victims' feelings matter. Once you have done this then they will be far more receptive to considering the victims of their behaviour and to entertaining the idea that their feelings matter too.

And with this comes the introduction of the idea that they might be locked into a victim-victimiser cycle- that their acting out as a result of being victimised, leads them to victimise others.

This is often the great 'lights-on' moment for so many abused teens. They begin to understand the source of their behaviour better and realise that they don't have to continue being victimised or continue to victimise others. They experience an empowerment surge as it dawns on them that they have the power to break the cycle. They subsequently find themselves in a mental space where they are no longer able to use their past experience as an excuse for their current negative behaviour. Instead their past experience becomes a reason to stop that behaviour.

Whether coming from a place of abuse or not, in helping teens wear their own victim shoes, you are teaching them how to draw on their own experience in order to help them wear the shoes of others- to empathise.

THE RIPPLE EFFECT:

TAKE THOSE SHOES FOR A WALK

So you've at least got them looking at the victims' shoes. The next step is to take them for a walk in them and to maybe realise that it is most likely that there is more than one pair of victim shoes they need to try on.

When considering how their actions affect others, it is so easy for the teen, and for you, their worker or parent, to miss the bigger picture. The victim of the assault is the person who has now got a black-eye right? Well yes, but so too is the family of the black-eye guy, the family of the aggressive teen, the rest of the community (be it school or local community) who are shaken by the assault. Do you see what I mean?

One great way of ensuring you and the teen get the whole picture is to use a Ripple Effect chart. (This can be seen on the following page and can be downloaded free from *www.teenagewhisperer.co.uk/teenanger*). It makes it very clear to see everyone who is affected by a behaviour and the impact on them physically, emotionally, psychologically and financially. You can even create a life size chart on the ground with some chalk and get the young person to actually stand in each segment and speak as if they are the people in question.

For those who are desperate to avoid even thinking about how their actions impact others, either through a deep

THE RIPPLE EFFECT

The Issue/Crime/Situation

Effect on self

- Physical
- Emotional/ Psychological
- Financial

Effect on other person

- Physical
- Emotional/ Psychological
- Financial

Effect on Your Family

Effect on Community & Friends

Effect on other person's family

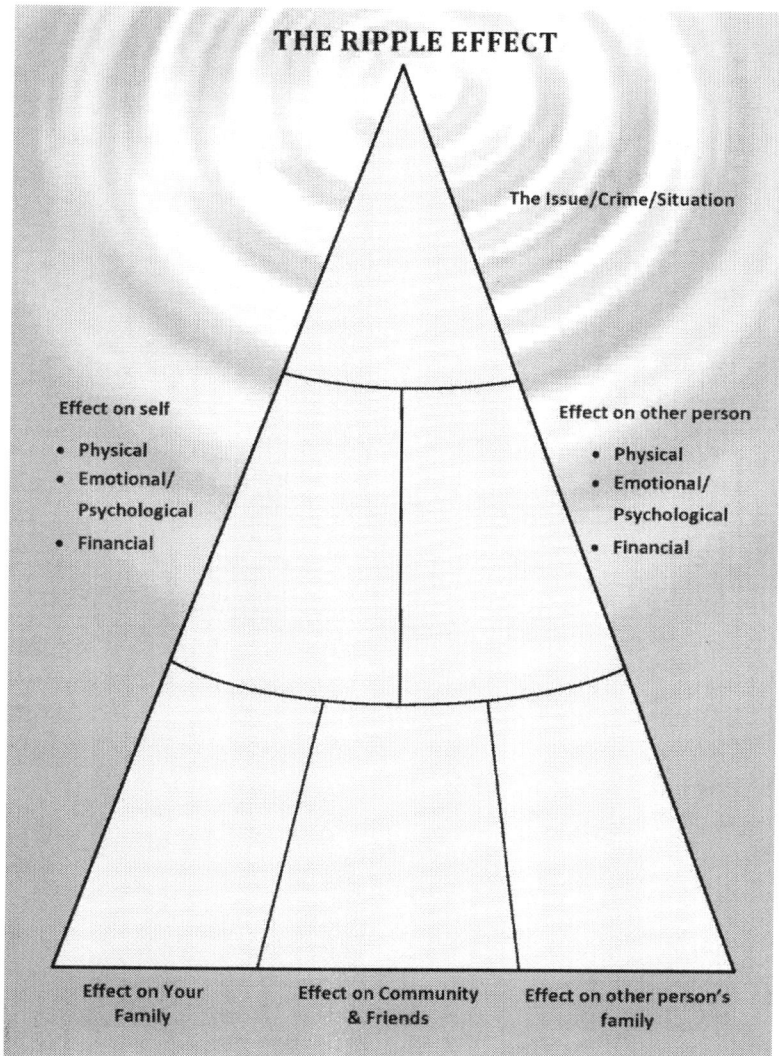

sense of shame, or through a strong desire to continue in their current behaviour or through fear of a personal emotional meltdown, a slightly different approach can be taken initially.

In these cases it can often be useful to look at third-person scenarios and victims first, to ease them into this way of thinking. Time and time again I have been able to connect with disengaged teens using this method- it's far less intimidating and stressful than placing them in the spotlight from the start. Trust can be built and the mental juices start to flow. So look at some clips from popular teen soaps, movies or even news items and complete the ripple effect chart for those scenarios.

For suggestions and links to potential material to use with your teens visit: *www.teenagewhisperer.co.uk/teenanger*

The ripple effect process is a great pill to the tendency to minimise the consequences of their behaviour or to come up with spurious justifications like "the insurance will cover it", or "it didn't really bother them, so it doesn't matter". It forces them to go deeper than one-liner brush-off statements and to think it all through.

Restorative justice conferencing is another commonly used and highly effective method of really getting teens to consider those they have harmed and to take responsibility for their actions. It is a tool that allows those who have been most affected by an incident to come together to share their feelings, describe how they have been affected and develop a plan to repair the harm done and prevent recurrence, and thereby find a positive way forward.

The facilitator first asks those who have caused harm to talk about what they did, what they were thinking about when they did it, and who they think may have been affected by their actions. The facilitator then asks victims

and their family members and friends to talk about the incident from their perspective, as well as how it affected them. The family and friends of the person who has caused harm are asked to do the same.

Finally the victim is asked what he or she would like to be the outcome of the conference. The response is discussed with everyone at the conference. When agreement is reached usually a simple contract is written and signed.

Restorative Justice Conferencing is a process increasingly being used in criminal justice, schools, care homes and the wider community and has been shown to reduce re-offending.

THE NECESSITY & POWER OF RECIPROCITY:

SHOW THEM THAT WE ARE ALL SHOES IN A SHOE SHOP

A natural corollary of looking into their own victim experiences and considering the effects of their actions on others is that they begin to view actions and consequences not in individualistic selfish terms but on larger scale, outward looking, community terms.

The next step is then to demonstrate that we are all in this thing called life together, whether we want to be or not. The best way to make it work for everyone, individually and together is to look out for one another and not just ourselves. It might seem obvious, but we are more alone and more vulnerable in isolation. If we are wholly individualistic we descend into dog-eat-dog-ism which means that we constantly have to watch our backs.

This often does not occur to teens. They are so caught up in the short-term personal gain of what they are doing, that they don't see the bigger picture of how their lack of care for others affects them detrimentally in the long run.

It is consequently vital that we teach our teens the importance of reciprocity- that if they want people to care about what happens to them, then they need to care about what happens to others. This is often framed in the terms of 'rights' and 'responsibilities'- that if you have the right not to be assaulted, for example, that you then have the responsibility to refrain from doing it to others. Do as you would be done by, or don't do what you don't want to happen to you.

Illustrating this process can be as simple as completing a worksheet like the one below. Blank copies of the following worksheets can be downloaded at *www.teenagewhisperer.co.uk/teenanger*

LOOKING IN, LOOKING OUT

My rights & desires	My responsibility
I want to feel safe	Don't make other people feel unsafe
I want to be treated like I matter	Treat others like they matter by listening to them, talking to them respectfully and politely

It seems almost monotonous and obvious, but sometimes it takes writing down the seemingly obvious for the message to get through.

You can also help them to make the connection between specific instances of their behaviour, how that violated the victim(s)'s rights and desires and what their responsibility is in light of this, using the worksheet on the following page.

When writing down what they did or said it is important to describe it precisely. If they said 'fuck off', write that down. If we 'tidy it up' with general terms like 'I swore at....'' then we are only helping them minimise their behaviour. Writing the graphic details down might make you uncomfortable, but that is because your social

BREAKING THE CYCLE

Behaviour	Rights & Desires Violated	My Responsibility
Called Mrs Foster a "fat bitch"	To be spoken to politely To be treated as if feelings do matter	Speak politely to others Consider other people's feelings when I say or do things
Mum always calling me "useless"	To feel loved and wanted To feel that I can do some things well To be noticed when I do well	Be encouraging to other people Cheer people on instead of taking the mick Notice the good stuff in other people, not just their faults

conscience is provoking a reaction in you. Sometimes it is only after an event, when it is being relived out of the heat of the moment, that people become aware of what their social conscience is telling them. Many a time I have completed this exercise and the teen who threw out offensive language in the heat of the moment, cowers or blushes with embarrassment when the exact words they used are looked at in the cold light of day.

By completing this exercise honestly and accurately you can help them more readily access behavioural controls like self-reflection and putting themselves in others' shoes, that do exist within them but that they have drowned out with the deafening thunder of their own emotions or just simply forgotten how to use.

This process can also be extremely beneficial for those who are locked into a victimised-victimiser cycle. They can explore how others' behaviour has affected them, directly or indirectly and what rights and desires of theirs they felt were violated. They can explore how the victimiser's overly narrow focus on their own feelings and needs may have caused them to fail to notice or care about the victim's needs. They can then commit to breaking the victimised-victimiser cycle by stating what they think their responsibilities to others in general are in light of this, to prevent them from doing the same to others.

In my experience, such a straightforward exercise like this can have profound effects. They realise their power as an individual to make positive changes in their own lives and in the lives of others. I believe that everyone at their core craves to feel that they matter and that they can make a difference and by doing this exercise they see that even as one person, they have the ability to be a force for good.

For those stuck in negative behaviour cycles, this can be a life-changing realisation and can be the quiet bulldozer that begins to break them out of those cycles.

READING EMOTION PROMPTERS:

SHOW THEM HOW TO TELL THE DIFFERENCE BETWEEN SHOES

Shoes come in all shapes, colours and sizes, some with Velcro, some with laces, some with zips and so on it goes. In general, adults find it pretty easy to tell the difference between shoes, like between a lady's high-heel shoe and a man's black work shoe (otherwise there could be some quite hilarious results in the morning).

There are as many shoes as there are human emotions and as many shoes as there are associated expressions on faces, body postures and tone of voice. Imagine if you could not tell the difference between your shoes- where the difference between a black high-heel and a man's black shoe were difficult to discern.

For many teens, telling the difference between emotions can be as difficult as that. As was discussed earlier, it might be that they are on the autistic spectrum or just that they find reading facial expressions, body language and tone of voice difficult. They may even have trained themselves to shut down their own emotions and their ability to read others' emotions as a means of self-preservation.

It then becomes a challenge for them to alter their behaviour in response to the bodily expressed emotions of others. While it might appear that they just don't care how the victim feels, it might just be that they have missed out on the physical prompts and don't realise the effect that their actions are having on the other person. For example, when getting angry and shouting they might fail to read the prompts that the other person is upset and that they are scared.

While these prompts don't stop everyone even when they consciously see them, for most they do have a behaviour curtailing effect. Without the ability to read this however, this fundamental element of behavioural control is lost.

It is consequently vital that they are given the opportunity to improve those skills. It can prevent them from inflicting harm on others, and potentially putting themselves in harm's way.

This can be achieved in several ways. Links to the most dynamic and interesting resources I have come across can be found at *www.teenagewhisperer.co.uk/teenanger*. Some of the items listed include:

The Facial Expressions Game

This interactive tool allows a player to experiment with the different effects of moving separate facial parts. In teaching someone how a face conveys emotion, you may choose to isolate one part, such as turning brows down to indicate disapproval, or up for surprise.

Interpersonal Communication- 'Emotions' short film

This consists of six minutes worth of picture and video examples of the six key emotions that are a part of interpersonal communication- joy, surprise, anger, disgust, sadness, fear. This is a far more interesting dynamic way to analyse facial expressions and the emotions attached than just looking at facial emotion photocards, although obviously low-tech is sometimes the only option!

Watch an episode of their favourite TV soap or drama

In the UK, I find Channel 4's teen soap, 'Hollyoaks', usually works well. After each scene, pause for a few minutes and discuss the emotions expressed, and what clues there were that led them to this conclusion- facial expression, body pose, tone of voice.

THE SHOES THAT HEAL

So the answer to getting teens to cover the distance from their behaviour to the impact site is all in the shoes. If we get them to walk in their own victim shoes, get them to walk in others, show them that we are all a community of shoes and how to tell the difference between them, then the journey becomes all the easier. It benefits society as a whole and it benefits them.

By developing empathy they end up feeling more engaged with the world, less alone and better able to connect positively with it. When involved in the process, the victims of their behaviour also feel more empowered, less fearful and better connected too. It's a liberating process for all and a walk worth taking.

-

OVERCOMING THE CHALLENGE OF DISENGAGEMENT

-

I WILL NOT LOOK

Go away. Just leave me alone. No, I don't want to be here. You're going to make me think about myself, interrogate myself, question my decisions, my 'consequential thinking' or lack of it. My actions are going to be scrutinised and you're going to tell me how I could have done it better. Just go away, go away...

'Why the opposition?', you ask, 'What's the problem? I'm just trying to help you make better decisions for yourself. You'll find it makes life easier for you, less complicated, less chaotic.'

No, I'm having none of it. You're just having a go, picking at me, making me feel more crap than I do already. No thanks, no f'in thanks.

You see, when you ask me to think about what I do and about my decisions, my actions, that's not what you're really asking. Well at least as far as I see it. You're not asking me to reassess what I've done, you're asking me to reassess who I am. You're not questioning my choices, you're questioning the very essence of me. If my decisions are bad, then I am bad. And I don't want to look at that reflection in the mirror.

I'm on a knife-edge as it is and if you push me to look I don't know what will happen. And that scares me, deep-down fibre of my bones scares me. So I'll run or I'll hide; quietly by not showing up or loudly beneath some rage, violence or insult. But I will not look. I will not look.

My sense of self is an impossibly fragile thing. I might look tough and hard, but like a snail's shell if I am stood on I will shatter into a million pieces, into shards of myself. And my sense of who I am is so impossibly entwined with my actions, my decisions, what has been done to me, what I have done to others. So to ask about all those things is to ask about me. And I will not tell. I will not tell.

I will not tell of the confusion, the pain, the hurt, the regret, the shame, the pride, the happiness, the sadness, the anger, the buzz, the release, the guilt, the mess that is me. The goodness, the badness, the beauty and the horror.

That is, until you show me, first and foremost, that I am more than my past decisions and actions. That my sense of self is not under threat when you ask me to think, to reflect, because I am more than what I did, more than the thought processes that led me there.

What I need to know before I will let you anywhere near me is that my life is a long series of paintings, representations of me in moments in time. Created with brushstrokes of decisions made, coloured with the paint of circumstance, and textured with the consequences of mine and other people's decisions.

But I also need to know that I am not a painting, a flimsy piece of canvas, millimetres thick. I need to know that one moment's representation of me does not have to be the representation of me for all time, the portrait that captures who I am forever. I am me, the painting is a painting.

A painting can't withstand relentless scraping off of layers of decisions, never-ending poking at the layers of circumstance; it will disintegrate. And if I think I am the painting then neither can I. But if you help me to see that there is more depth to me, more than the layers of paint, that I have a core that exists separately to the painting of me, then the scraping, the exploring of the painting isn't nearly so intimidating.

I am then exploring the meaning of the painting, rather than the meaning of me, considering why I chose black over green, why I chose to scratch the canvas with the blunt end of the brush rather than the soft. I can discuss what I like and what I don't, show the bits that someone else painted for me and how that affected the other parts. Yes it will affect my understanding of me, but the me, the real me stays intact. I am analysing a moment in time, not the fundamental core of me.

I can do this without fear of being crushed because I am the artist, not the painting. I can deal with the pain of the previous portraits exactly because I am an artist and because I can paint another. There is hope in the possibility of future canvases. I can make better brushstrokes, better colour choices, have better techniques. I can bring the best out of me rather than the worst and display it on my new canvas, for all to see.

You then show me that the reason why we look at a painting is not to condemn, but to help us create anew, to grow, to improve, to learn. By critically analysing my previous choices in any one of my previous portraits I can see how each decision, each circumstance, each perception of myself led it to be the painting it turned out to be. I learn, and then I move on. My life becomes fluid; I escape a particular representation of me, in a particular time, in a particular place and I rework it.

I use parts from the old that I want in the new. Include the bits I'm proud of and re-render the bits I'm not. What was in the foreground before may now be in the background, or what I once viewed as dark may be reconceived in a lighter, more hopeful way. And I can try new techniques with confidence because I can always try again if that particular portrait doesn't work out. Because I am me, and the painting is a painting. We are closely linked but we are not one and the same.

You need to help me see all this. That just because I have made mistakes does not make me a mistake. It was maybe just a bad choice of colour, of brush or maybe someone shoved me while I was trying to paint. Or maybe the mixing of colours and layers on the canvas made an ugly colour I didn't intend.

If I summon up the courage to look, then I can seek to understand, to learn, and to get better. I can seek to take responsibility for my choices and I can absolve myself of the responsibility when the decision or circumstance was not of my making. Whatever the issue, if I look, I can better understand. I can learn from my and others' mistakes and create something better. I can paint the best of me.

The expression of me is not one canvas, it's a never-ending creative process. The act of painting is never done. Show me that you too are constantly painting, that you are not a completed work of art either. That way the humanity of your current portrait and mine is revealed and we connect as artists, constantly striving to learn, to paint better, to reconceptualise our pasts and create better futures. It is in looking, however painful, that we finally learn to see. To see that we are more than a representation in time and that we have untold potential for future works of art.

'HOW DO I FEEL?'
ARE YOU CRAZY?

You know one way of guaranteeing that I don't talk to you about anything? Ask me straight, 'how do you feel?' or 'how does that make you feel?'

I'll tell you how asking that question makes me feel- it makes me feel that you can go take a long walk off a short plank. 'How do I feel?' What a joke.

Do you not get it? Half the time I have absolutely no idea how I feel. I can feel ten emotions in ten minutes, some of them contradicting each other. I can't makes sense of it all. And even if I can make some sense of it in my own mind, I have no way of knowing how to express it.

Asking me to tell you how I feel is sometimes a bit like asking someone to tell you how to tie their laces. You know how to do it, how to physically do it, but you just can't tell someone how to do it. You have to show them. And that's what I do a lot of the time. I'll show you I'm angry at the abuse I've experienced by being aggressive. I'll show you I'm upset and need some space by colourfully telling you to get lost. I'll show you how crap I feel about myself by making other people feel small. I'll show you I have intolerable emotional pain by cutting myself. And most of the time I will be able to show you how I feel before I even know in my head how I feel or why I feel that way. The information is in there somewhere, I just don't know how to mentally access it, to put it into words.

So don't go asking me straight up how I feel and particularly when I barely know you. I'll just think you have no idea, are not worth talking to, listening to, having anything to do with. You'll be nothing more than a nosey clueless therapist, worker or teacher. And it's not just us, the gals and lads who have had a tough time, the ones who are acting out, who find these 'how do you feel?' questions stupid.

Most teen boys on the planet will tell you that directly asking them about feelings in general, and theirs in particular is just about the most embarrassing exposing thing you can do to them. You might as well ask them to stand on the table and strip naked. I know where I'd tell you to shove that idea.

Feelings, talking about them, writing about them is something that comes way more naturally to girls, they even like to do it. Not all girls, but a lot of them. To be fair, some girls who get in loads of trouble are a bit more like lads; they often aren't into talking about emotions and stuff either. But in general girls know how to pump the verbal emotional well, and sometimes too well. Ask them how they feel and they are way more likely to welcome and answer the question than squirm in revulsion.

Yeah, I totally do need to get to grips with my feelings and how they affect what I do, but not by being asked in this way. I ain't no emotional well-pumper. Ask me how I feel, even in a spirit of helpful understanding, and I will not gush, far from it. In fact, all you'll get me to do is vandalise the pump so that nothing will come out.

But there is a way to get me to at least let trickles come out, which will probably grow to a reasonable sort of flow. It's about understanding how I cope with life and coming at it from my angle.

If I'm in front of you because of my behaviour, then I am clearly a 'doer' in trying to cope with my life, rather than a talker. I'll clobber other kids to try and make me feel better; I'll drink or take drugs to try and forget; I'll self-harm. I won't go and talk to my mates, to a teacher, a youth worker, a relative. This is mostly to do with not wanting to expose myself, make myself feel more vulnerable and insecure than I do already. So I'll try to cope in other 'doing' ways, often with bad results.

What you need to show me is that sometimes doing is not enough, and sometimes I do need to talk in order to break the cycle of my actions. You need to show me that there is no shame, no judgement, no need to feel scared in doing that. But you need to do it in a way that respects my inclination to 'do' rather than talk about feelings.

Tell me that I need to talk about my feelings, and I will show you exactly what silence sounds like. Show me how I can talk and how I can express feelings without losing my sense of dignity and you will hear my voice.

SO HOW DO YOU GET ME TO TALK?

When trying to get to the bottom of why I am behaving in a particular way, explore the triggers for the behaviour, not the feelings triggers but the 'what happened?' triggers. Like Dad shouting at me, or another kid taunting me, or just being ignored.

Instead of asking me how I feel, ask me what I did. Remember, my natural inclination is to 'do'. I cope by doing, so I am far more likely to talk about doing than feeling.

You'll never get me to move from doing and not talking about how I feel, to not doing and talking about how I feel. That's too much of a quantum leap. It's a bit like asking a snake to tap dance. It just isn't going to happen.

By asking what I did, I will start to talk, and you will end up exploring my emotions, but in an indirect non-threatening way. As part of me telling you what I did, some expression of feeling will come in, reasons as to why I did what I did, the emotions underlying the actions. You can end up having a conversation something like this:

'So what happened yesterday?'

'Well I punched him, didn't I?'

'Why did you punch him?'

'He just wouldn't shut up about my shoes.'

'... so you were angry?'

'Too right I was. Stupid dick.'

'What was he saying about your trainers?'

'He said they were crap and did my Mummy choose them?'

'Why didn't you like this?'

'He made me look stupid, made me look like a baby or some'in'.'

'So you don't like it when people make you look small?'

'Yeah I guess... I hate that, man... It totally sucks.'

Does anyone else make you look or feel small?

'Mmm, I guess when my Dad yells at me.'

You see? Not one question directly asking me how I feel. You just let me talk, reflect back what I have said and enquire further with the right questions. If I think you are enquiring into what I do, rather than directly at what I feel, then I am way more likely to talk and in the course of us talking, if I don't feel threatened or nosed upon, I will gradually spill the beans. The beans of why I do what I do, the emotions that motivate me.

Reflecting back what I have said and asking the right questions makes me feel like you understand me, you 'get me'. And that is the kind of person I can talk to, someone who doesn't make me feel like I am standing on the table, starkers. You show me that talking about emotions doesn't have to be scary and emotionally dangerous for me. I can keep my dignity and my emotional clothes on. It's often a stealthy operation. I often won't realise we are talking about how I feel until after the conversation, if at all. I'm just talking about my life and what I do.

And you know what? If you talk to me about this stuff in this way, while doing something else at the same time, like playing cards, I am even more likely to spill the beans. For one thing, you are distracting me from what we're talking about. Remember I'm a doer, that's why I'm in the pickle I'm in, so get me doing the 'doing' that comes naturally, to distract me from the fear of what doesn't come naturally, the talking.

Even people who like to talk often do something at the same time. When was the last time you had a chat in a boring room with nothing to distract you at least slightly, so that you could look down or momentarily focus on something other than the topic of conversation? People tend to meet with people while doing something- drinking coffee, eating some food, going for a walk or playing sport. And when you've got a difficult conversation to have, the activity becomes so important. It reduces the pressure, the tension.

So why would it be any different for me? I don't want to get the special treatment of your visual spotlight. It doesn't work for you, so why on earth would it work for me?

If we must sit in a room, at least chat with me while playing a board game, doodling or make sure there is something I can fiddle with like a stress ball. Better still play pool, where we can constantly move about. Your ability to get me and other people who are extremely reluctant or hostile to engage with this process, to open up, to talk, depends on it.

As I said before, even though I am a 'doing coper' I will often need to talk to break the cycle of coping badly. Precisely because I am a 'doing coper' rather than a natural 'talker coper', talking as a single, long-term coping strategy for me probably won't work, particularly once our time together has ended. Yes, encourage and help me to find someone who I feel I can talk to, but you know what will work a whole load better? Help me to get involved in a constructive activity that will help me to cope. Help me to be a constructive 'doing coper' rather than a self-destructive one.

De-stressing is a pretty major need for most of us so find something that does exactly that. For some that might mean joining a craft group, others a sports team, others just taking their mind off their troubles by helping others with theirs. And you know what? I will probably find my support network right there- friends, role models, people who will come to care about me. And the end result- people I might be able to talk to if I feel the need, for the times when the just 'doing' isn't enough.

So in trying to get me to address the underlying emotional causes of my outward behaviour you need to respect that I am naturally a 'doing coper' rather than a 'talking feeler' and adapting your approach accordingly. Yes I need to learn to address my feelings, but you need to show me that I don't need or have to emotionally strip-off and that there are a variety of ways of exploring and talking about emotion. If you want to hear me, you've got to let me talk in the way I think and talk. To ask me to do anything else is only to ask me to stop talking.

'I HATE YOU':
A POWERFUL TOOL FOR CHANGE

It's all your fault. All your f'in fault. You can't just leave me alone, leave me to do my thing can you? You have to meddle, stick your nose in where it's not wanted. And I hate you for it. I absolutely bloody hate you for it.

Everyone's at it. You're at it, teachers are at it, social workers, doctors, nurses, therapists, care home workers, you're all in it together making my life an f'in living hell. If you'd just leave me, my family, my mates alone I'd be just fine. Thinking you know better about me and my life than I do, f'in cheek.

I hate you, you hate me. Well this is going to work well isn't it?

"I'm getting that you're angry with me? Or is it social workers/school/the Youth Offending Team in general? What's winding you up?'

Woah, hang on a minute? They actually care that I'm well peeved? Scratch that, they've even noticed I'm peeved?! I think we're in for an interesting ride...

Immediately, I'm paying attention. This is different, real different. And so it begins... the beginning of me learning not to hate you. Me learning that maybe you do want to help. Me learning something about myself. Me moving past this rage that I have against you, your organisation, life and people in general, and actually engaging. Me changing stuff, changing my thinking, my attitudes, my behaviour. Me becoming different, real different.

So what makes the difference? How do you harness this powerful hate and turn it into something constructive? What gets me from this place of hate to a place of change?

You noticing. Even if my thinking is based on misconceptions about you and your organisation, the fact that you even notice that I am feeling something negative about you and consider it of importance to mention means more than you probably realise. By noticing, you acknowledge my emotion. You don't necessarily agree, but you recognise its existence. You acknowledge my anger and hurt at injustice I feel has been done to me by you or your organisation, sometimes correctly and sometimes incorrectly perceived. Suddenly I exist.

You allowing me to feel as I feel. Most of the time when I'm getting pretty pissed about a situation people try and shut me down, get me to be quiet. All this says to me is that I'm not allowed to be angry, not allowed to be annoyed. That my feelings about a situation don't count for much. But my feelings do count, they count very much.

While the factual basis of them may be a bit dodgy, while I may be viewing the situation with immaturity, naivety, with a blindness to the character flaws of significant people around me and how that has led me to here, while my expression may leave a lot to be desired, I feel as I feel. Before trying to do anything else with me, you have to allow me to feel as I feel. It doesn't happen often.

Yes, it might not be the right moment for me to vent, like in the middle of class but you can still allow me to feel as I feel without allowing me to disrupt everyone and everything else. Telling me in a calm manner, "Now is not the right time to discuss this. Please go outside, take a moment and then we can discuss what is going on."

It's then much harder for me to be angry at you because you haven't dismissed my emotion, you've just rejected the timing. Once I've calmed down I will be in a better position to allow a two-way discussion about why I'm angry and why I might not be expressing myself in the best way. You might not be able to have this discussion with me five minutes later, either because I haven't calmed down or because you have other young people to work with. As long as you verbally commit to actually exploring the issue as soon as is practically possible, I will know you are wanting to listen.

It is precisely because you first acknowledge my emotion and provide the right physical and emotional environment for me to explore and better express myself, that I realise you are different and maybe worth giving a chance. Rather than shutting me down, you let me open up.

You're listening. You are always trying to 'get me'. Even if I am thinking that all social workers are scum, all teachers are dickheads, you think I am important enough to try and understand. You try and understand it all from my point of view. That empathy that so many think I lack- well you always show me what it looks like.

You let me tell my story of how I got here, along with all the misconceptions I have, my bendings of the truth. By letting me tell my story, judgements aside, you open yourself to learning how I tick and that means that you are always in the best position to work out what you need to do to help me. So the stuff we talk about, the things we do always seem relevant to me. Me as an individual, me with my very own tailored suit of help.

You 'get' that I don't 'get' me. I don't understand myself- why I think what I think, why I feel what I feel, why I do what I do. I don't 'get' how my thoughts, emotions and actions influence one another. Half the time I don't even really know what I think and feel- I'm in survival mode, operating on a purely instinctual level.

That's why instead of understanding how my actions might have affected my situation and how my thoughts and emotions fuelled those, or how others actions have got me here, or what I even felt in the first place, I do the obvious thing and blame you and your organisation for getting me here. By blaming you, I have all the understanding I think I need. It is your fault, that's it. No change is needed here, ball is in your court.

But you see past my invective and don't make the classic mistake...

You don't try and change something that I don't already understand. So often workers see my anger at them and their organisations and they label me with 'anger management issues', 'lack of personal responsibility for actions', a 'retaliatory aggressive attitude'. They then very efficiently launch into a one-size-never-fits-all anger management or consequential thinking program. They try and teach me new approaches, new tools. But you 'get' that this is pointless. You 'get' that you can't get me to think differently, to feel differently, to behave differently until I first 'get' what I am feeling and thinking and doing right now. You totally 'get' that I can't change something that I don't understand in the first place, into something different. That has to come later.

You always start exactly where I am at. So I'm here right now and I'm angry at you and at your organisation. So you work with that.

I blame you and your organisation for being in court, for being in this hell-hole of a children's home, for having to be at this dumb-ass appointment, for having to change schools.... And so instead of brushing this aside and trying to 'achieve' something else with me, you embrace this as a learning experience for both of us. I'm so caught up in my emotion against you right now, I can't be thinking of anything else. So you work with that, that's what I'm bothered about right now. That's where we can connect.

So you help me unpick it, and in doing so start to learn more about me, and also help me to begin to understand what and how I feel, how thinking, emotions and actions interact, about perceptions and misconceptions. And as I get it off my chest I begin to thaw. Hell, I'm talking to you which is a minor miracle in itself. You're beginning to 'get' me', I'm beginning to 'get' me.

You help me unpack misconceptions, to see a different perspective. I begin to see that just because people think and say that social workers are meddling scum, doesn't make it true. That just because I have been treated unfairly by some teachers and this has caused me great upset, does not mean that all teachers are unfair. I then learn that I should not be driven by this emotional memory of betrayal, of unfairness, to treat all teachers badly, that I can put my thinking into play to try and control this emotional response.

Just the fact that you are right here, destroying all my beliefs about people who do your job, people in your organisation, gives me my first insight into the fact that my thinking isn't always right. That my emotionally driven responses aren't always based on fact, but often on misconceptions, on faulty belief systems, on blanket judgements. And so you have something to build on, I'm beginning to let you in.

You help me to reconnect with my thinking, my feeling, my behaviour and help put me back in control. Instead of being at the mercy of myself, I actually stand a chance of being in control of myself. And that feels good. You think I'm out of control, well deep down I kind of know it too. And when I begin to get that feeling of being back in control again, I don't want to lose it. I kind of wake up to myself and my attitude changes. I hate less, I feel less squashed by life and I begin to feel that maybe I do have the ability to change. What once seemed impossible to me now seems very possible.

And then you start cookin'. Once I'm in this 'rethink' mode where I feel I have possibilities, then I am way more interested in any focused interventions to deal with my anger, peer pressure, substance abuse, whatever my issues are. Connect with me, connect me with myself and things start changing.

You just have to start at the beginning, the very beginning and want to learn about me, from me. You've got to 'get' me before you get me. Often the best way to achieve this is to seize on the very thing that you think destroys any chance of me successfully working with you- my anger towards you. It's a powerful thing, but if you walk into it rather than away from it a real sparking connection occurs and that energy can be converted into movement for change.

THE PAPER EXCHANGE

...because sometimes it is not just teens who disengage

I'm a label, a sticker, a scrawl on a file
A person lost in the paper mile
That runs from birth to right here now
You know me but you don't and I'll tell you how

My name spells trouble, it's written ahead
In the assessments, the reports, the letters you've read
You know my circumstance, my life, my woe
But any deeper you just won't go

All you see is an impression, a view of me
Without affording me the privilege of being free

Free to break from my past and start afresh
Cos you pegged me already before our first sess

You decided who I was and what I'm about
Neutered me, silenced me, labelled me 'lout'
You didn't listen, you didn't enquire
And consequently threw me on the 'unworkable' fire

All I ask for is a slate, clean each time
So I'm not reduced to a pointless mime
Where you decide I'm a goner before I've begun
And I flick you the finger and break out in a run

And you write your report, your assessment, my life
Bound up with the string of the imaginary strife
That you thought I would bring to my sessions with you
That rendered useless our relationship glue

The glue that would have led to trust and to change
To breaking down strongholds and rebuilding again
But instead I am captive, folded in a large piece of card
Of my past, preconceptions and the fact I appear 'hard'

And my name on that file circulates once more
It gets transported through yet another organisational
door

Where another professional opens it up
And decides I'm impossible while they sip from their cup

It isn't intentional, it isn't malicious
It just has an end result that's pernicious
That stops you from seeing me, listening, connecting
One of us hits the button, we end up ejecting

So please remember my file is just paper, words and views
Informing of facts and pertinent issues
But if you want to know me let me tell you my tale
That's the view you've got to work with, if progress will prevail

So please stop shuffling the paper me around
And stop, talk and listen and then I might just be found
The person in 3D with feelings, with capacity to change
Just give me the time, the effort, the opportunity to exchange.

WHAT'S THE POINT?
MAGICAL TOOLS AND RESOURCE RABBIT HOLES

A worksheet is just a piece of a paper, a group is just a collection of people, an app is 0s and 1s and a DVD is a clear disc of plastic with a thin metallic covering. This we should never forget.

It is so easy to imbue all the above with some supernatural power to get the job done, to teach something, to change behaviour. If we use the tools, we're no fools. We're cutting edge, we're interesting and we're dynamic. If we use any of the above or the latest 'thing' we become a model of good practice, the worker that all managers point to as some practice genius.

But be warned, we can use all the tools and be real big fools. We can be left with a teen or group of teens who haven't changed their thinking or actions one iota, who haven't taken on board anything.

We can be left wondering, how did these tools go so wrong? How did these tools, these programs that looked so great, so interesting, lead to nothing? Why does it seem like we haven't moved forward?

It's because we missed the point.

We picked up that resource with some dangerous assumptions in our minds, preconceived ideas as to how this was going to work:

WE THOUGHT THE TOOL WAS THE ANSWER, NOT A WAY OF FINDING THE ANSWER

Because it is so easy to assess that someone has a problem, anger management say, and to find a tool to 'fix it', we think our assessment of them is over. The reality is that seeing the generic problem is usually pretty easy. What we can forget is that we need to interrogate further to understand why this is an issue for them- the tools should be a means of helping us do this, not the answer in itself. They should also help us work out what new strategies and tools our teen can usefully employ to help them overcome their issue and the way it presents for them.

The key thing to remember is that in all of this we should always be thinking. We should always be clear in our own minds as to what piece of information we are looking for, what clarity we are needing when we use that workbook or watch that DVD. Other information beyond what we are looking for will probably emerge, but we should always have a purpose in mind when we start each task, each activity we embark on. We are not using the tool or resource because it happens to be there with the same title as the problem we have diagnosed in the teen, we are going deeper and using the tool to help us understand and to help us help them.

WE USED THE TOOLS BLINDLY AND SURRENDERED OUR OWN JUDGEMENT

We always followed each page of that consequential thinking workbook. We always watched every section of that peer pressure DVD. We always used that iPad app with every kid because they loved using it. And we always did group work with anti-social kids cos it would teach them social skills amongst other things. But we didn't question whether that was appropriate. We didn't consider whether all parts of the program, the DVD, the book were relevant to them. We bought into the resource or the tool, hook-line-and-sinker and inadvertently turned our brains, our thinking, our judgement off.

WE FORGOT THAT EVERY TEEN IS DIFFERENT, EVEN IF THEY HAVE THE SAME PROBLEM

The roots of issues will not be the same for all, the methods of unpacking the issue and 'solving' or 'coping' with it will not be the same either. So a one-size fits all anger management intervention, for example, will not work for all. It might work for some, but certainly not all.

So whipping out the same tool will not always work. For some a totally different tool will be needed. Or it might just mean that we need to tailor our usual set of tools to work for the individual(s) sat in front of us.

Using a resource with the expectation that not all of it will be used is a healthy mindset to start with. It keeps us awake to whether all of it is relevant to all our teens.

WE FORGOT HOW DISENGAGING IRRELEVANCY IS

When engaging teens in the first place, and keeping them engaged can be an uphill struggle, spending time on irrelevancies is a dangerous thing. If they don't see the point of it, then there is actually little point. It has to be relevant to them or it and you become an irrelevance.

While many authors of resources would argue that you need to maintain a programme's integrity and not 'chop it up', I would argue that our practice integrity and our ability to keep them engaged is more important. We need to trust ourselves and our professional judgement, our ability to 'read' the teen in front of us and cater for them. We need to allow ourselves to think for ourselves and not to hand over the reins to someone who has never met the teen and has no grasp of their particular issues like we do.

WE BLAMED DISENGAGEMENT ON THE TEEN OR THE TOOLS, RATHER THAN CONSIDERING OUR ROLE

They don't see the point of what we are doing with them, it doesn't seem relevant, so they kick off and verbally and/or physically let us know what they think of our tools. Or they sit there with a look of imminent death plastered all over their faces; yes, 'tortured by boredom' is a certifiable cause of death for teens.

Most likely we'll reflect and lay blame for non-engagement at their door- 'they just weren't ready', 'I won't be able to achieve anything with them until their attitude changes'. This is particularly likely when we have had success using this tool with other young people already.

Occasionally we might question the tool, 'maybe it's not pitched quite right for them'.

There may be some truth in all of the above, but if at the core we haven't been fully engaging with the tool as a tool and have instead been using it as a comprehensive solution, we have probably been running solely on a standby power setting. We need to ensure we are keeping our investigative brains fully switched on, fully powered-up. That way our tools become more useful for us in helping them, and our work with teens stays relevant for them. If we are not mentally engaging with the tool as a tool then the chances are they aren't fully engaging with it either.

It might be that the problem is not the teen, and it's not the tool either. It just might be that we are trying to bang the nail in with the handle end of the hammer. It damages the handle and it most likely bends the nail so it won't go in. We have to consider our roles as carpenters and whether our use of the hammer is the problem and whether we need to wield it more effectively.

WE THOUGHT THAT THE COMPLETION OF TASKS MEANT ENGAGEMENT, POINTED TOWARDS CHANGE

Non-engagement doesn't have to look like a swearing or furniture throwing competition. Non-engagement can seem far more compliant than we initially realise. Just as we can go through the motions, producing the tools without a second thought, so can teens. They can unthinkingly complete tasks, think 'what's the point?' and still get on with it and not really take the info, 'the lesson' on board.

This can be seen as progress in itself for a teen who never completes any task, but in terms of engagement with the particular subject of the intervention, this is not what progress looks like. The first we know about their disengagement is when we are dismayed to discover they have been out at the weekend and done exactly what they usually do, clearly not having taken on board any of the work you have been doing with them.

WE CONFUSED ENGAGEMENT WITH THE MEDIUM AS ENGAGEMENT WITH THE ISSUE

Give a kid an electronic device and it's like a bee round a honeypot. Give a kid who likes to hide from life a screen to hide in, television, iPad, mobile, whatever and he'll hide in it. So when we see them engrossed we have to ask ourselves what they are engrossed in and not just assume it's the issue/ subject matter.

Particularly for the most disengaged, using electronics of one sort or another can be a great way to get them to engage with the subject matter that they'd rather avoid. But we have to engage them with the content as well as the delivery method.

For example, watching DVDs with teens can be extremely useful for stimulating conversation about a topic, getting them to consider an issue in the context of other people at a time when they are not ready to talk directly about themselves. But just watching the DVD is not enough; just looking at other people is not enough. We have to move it on to consideration of themselves if any progress is going to be made.

WE DIDN'T DUMP THE TOOL WHEN WE REALLY NEEDED TO AND PREVENTED OURSELVES FROM MOVING FORWARD

Everyone's raving about it. It sits on the office shelf and seemingly glows, reflecting all the accolades it has received. Or it's been 'shown to work', entered the shiny halls of being evidenced as best practice. Problem is we can end up thinking 'I just don't like it... it just doesn't work... but why does everyone else like it? Is there something wrong with me and the way I practise?'

I'm all for trying tools that have been shown to 'work'. It's important that these evaluations take place otherwise we can end up just shooting in the dark. But again, we have to be so careful to persist in paying attention to our own judgement and our ability to assess what works for an individual teen and what works for us.

We all have our own methods, our own approaches, our own voices. It is important that we constantly seek to evolve, to improve and that necessarily involves trying new 'proven' methods and tools out, even if it does seem awkward or different at first. But there has to come a point when we make our own assessment of whether a tool works 'with' us or not, whether it ultimately helps us to help a teen.

If we have ensured that we haven't fallen foul of any of the assumptions or common mistakes above, and we have given it a good run, then sometimes we have to conclude for ourselves that it is not for us, even if that does go against what the majority thinks or the research says. That doesn't mean that the resource is universally unhelpful, it's just that it isn't right for all people in all places.

The beauty of accepting this, is that it frees us up to move on, to look for something better that will work for us and our teens. Sometimes, as I discovered, it can often lead you down the road of designing your own program, your own resource, your own toolkit. Sometimes it's entirely unique, sometimes it's a mash-up of the other resources out there. Whatever it is, it frees us to be more helpful and that is the core of our work.

'What works' is great as a starting point, but we have to be careful not to let it be our endpoint. We have to be mindful that what it provides in consistency, it can stifle in creativity, in independent forward thinking. Our independent thinking could be the next big 'what works', but only if we allow ourselves to wander, where appropriate, from the beaten track.

In all of this, in everything we do, we need to be clear about what we are doing. We need to be clear about what the point of an intervention is and why we are using particular tools and resources. We also need to be continually assessing whether the intervention overall and the tools we have employed are working; are they helping or hindering?

If we do this, then it is less likely that we will be led astray by the mistaken assumptions about the tools that we use. It is far less likely that we will fall down the resource rabbit hole, leaving teens wondering where the hell we have gone and what the hell we are doing down there, before deciding that they are bored waiting and they carry on... as usual.

THEY PUT ME IN A GROUP

They put me in a group, but I would not talk

They put me in a group, I was there but I wasn't

They put me in a group expecting sharing, enlightenment, support

They put me in a group and instead I battened down the hatches.

They put me in a group and I said what they wanted to hear

They put me in a group, my mouth moved but my thoughts did not

They put me in a group until the buttons got pressed and I kicked off

They put me in a group and nothing changed.

They put me in a group due to time and budget

constraints

They put me in a group cos that's just what they do

They put me in a group cos then they were doing something

They put me in a group, labelled, diagnosed, to be cured.

They put me in a group and it plain didn't work

They put me in a group and it became further proof

They put me in a group on the way out the door

They put me in a group, but never saw or knew me.

They put me in a group and wondered why the words did not flow

 I stuttered, I stuttered, I floundered, I fell...

I needed the I, the me, the quiet tranquillity

Of knowing you listened, you heard, you explored

You knew how I ticked, the trauma, the triggers

Before putting me in a room where all I could envisage were sniggers

I needed to share first, to one before another

To feel safe and secure like talking to a brother

Before I'd have the courage, see the purpose and point

Of groups, of sharing, strategies, turning up to the joint

And when I walked out the group room I was not again alone

You were there for a chat, to reflect, to further hone

The things I had learned, discussed and shared

If nothing else to see how I'd fared.

They put me in a group cos it was the right thing for me,

They put me in a group at the right time when I was ready

They put me in a group without leaving me stranded at the door

They put me in a group and I kept wanting to come back for more.

They put me in a group understanding the I

They put me in a group understanding the why

They put me in a group and help became mutual

They put me in a group and I started to find my future.

They put me in a group and I felt safe to think

They put me in a group with a well from which to drink

They put me in a group to rebuild anew

And it all started with the I and the understanding you.

Group work is a valuable method of engaging with young people when used at the right time, for the right issues, with teens who are ready. Some teens successfully dive into group work, engage, contribute and learn with relatively little extra individual support. In fact, some can open up more in a group setting than in one-on-one sessions.

Others, however, can struggle due to a number of things including deeply personal and painful individual issues, mental health issues, due to other young people in the group that they know, or because they are more of an introvert than an extrovert, more readily able to share on an individual rather than a group basis. They might say nothing, they might deliberately sabotage and disrupt the group, or they might go through the motions of saying what you want to hear.

As in everything, we have to be aware that what works for one teen may not work for another. So rather than reaching for the 'unworkable' stamp when a teen does not successfully engage in group work, we need to consider whether we have really seen and understood an individual's needs and have asked them to do more than they are currently able to.

OVERCOMING RESISTANCE TO CHANGE: THE STRONGEST ARGUMENT YOU CAN MAKE IS NOT TO

Most teens love to resist anything that you might have to suggest to them. Arguing with adults is a daily sport that they love to engage in, particularly when it concerns you trying to make them do something they don't want to do. They do it at home, they do it at school, they do it with social workers, they do it with youth justice workers. No-one is exempt.

When the change that you want them to make involves some seriously damaging behaviour, either to themselves, others or both, and you want them to stop, then the stakes are really high. It might be aggressive behaviour, alcohol or drug abuse, risky sexual behaviour or criminal activity, to name a few. You want to literally shake some sense into them before it's too late and they end up doing something with dire consequences.

With out of control anger the stakes are always high. Damage, either physical or emotional is always a consequence of the uncurtailed version of this emotion. The victims are others, themselves, walls, doors, windows. The victims are also those around them having to deal with the aftermath of an episode, whether it was an eruption or a more passive aggressive stirring of the life pot.

Police, school exclusions and general alienation result, whether it be alienation on a smaller scale from the school community or from peers, or on a larger scale involving incarceration. Whatever the scale, life options diminish and doors close rather than open.

At a time in their lives when the world should be their oyster, instead their world becomes an increasingly smaller oppressive prison. Unless they turn their behaviour around, a life built around strong respectful relationships will increasingly elude them, along with the happiness that everyone so desperately craves.

We, looking on can see this. They, in the midst of this, invariably find it difficult to see the bigger picture. We want them to see it as quickly as possible, so that options and real happiness can be theirs, but the clock is ticking. With the tick, tock in the background the temptation is to lecture, even in the nicest possible way, to highlight the dangers, to tell them why they should stop.

Problem is, you argue your case, and they argue back, or they just tell you to get lost and 'win' the argument by ignoring you altogether. You're exhausted, they're exhausted. You talked, they didn't listen. They talked, you didn't listen. You think they're foolhardy, they think you have no clue. And what is the end result of these exchanges? Usually absolutely nothing. They still don't want to change.

So what can be done? You don't want to stand by and watch them self-destruct. So is there a way you can encourage change without ending up with complete disengagement or relentless arguing?

THE STAGES OF CHANGE MODEL

In understanding resistance to change and how to overcome it, it is important to understand the very thing that we are trying to achieve with them from beginning to end- the process of change. If we pick it apart it amounts to the mental stages, processes and actions that any person needs to go through prior to making a change, while enacting a change and while maintaining that change.

Prochaska and DeClemente's (1983) model of the stages of change very clearly encapsulates the thinking and action processes that a person will go through on the road to new behaviour.

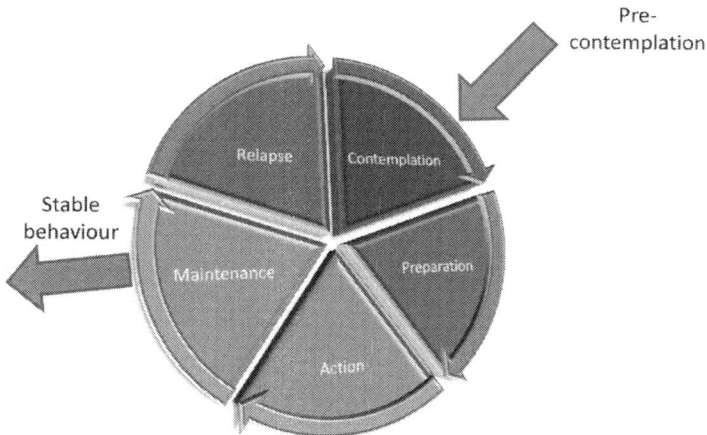

In the process of change a person moves from being uninterested, unaware or unwilling to make a change (precontemplation), to considering a change (contemplation), to deciding and preparing to make a change. Genuine, determined action is then taken and, over time, attempts to maintain the new behaviour occur. Relapses are almost inevitable and become part of the process of working toward lifelong change. When the change in behaviour has been maintained for a significant period of time and the individual no longer has to actively attend to the task of maintenance it can be said that they have achieved the change and exit the cycle. Some never fully reach this stage as they feel that there is always some potential for relapse and they constantly have to actively maintain their new behaviour.

PRECONTEMPLATION STAGE

During the precontemplation stage, people do not even consider changing. They either do not view their behaviour as a problem; they have tried to change it previously and failed so decide that change is pointless and do not consider it an option anymore; or it has not even occurred to them that there is an alternate way of behaving.

CONTEMPLATION STAGE

During the contemplation stage, people are ambivalent about changing. Giving up an enjoyed behaviour, or behaviour that has perceived benefits causes them to feel a sense of loss despite the perceived gain. During this stage, people assess barriers (e.g., time, expense, hassle, fear, perceptions of personal inadequacy) as well as the benefits of change as they try to decide whether they want to make the change.

For example, for a teen with control anger issues the perceived loss of control and associated feelings of vulnerability have to be outweighed by the benefits of employing new more positive ways of interacting with others before change becomes a possibility.

Or for those whose anger is rooted in traumatic experiences, the process of exploring and understanding those experiences will hopefully move them on to a point where they decide they don't want to react to their past in the same way anymore and that there is more to be gained from trying out new behaviours.

DETERMINATION / PREPARATION STAGE

During the determination stage, people prepare to make a specific change. For example if someone is preparing or determining to exercise more, they might buy some trainers.

In the case of a teen with anger issues, they might start engaging with and practising new coping strategies privately in sessions with you. Strategies such as asking for timeouts and walking away from potential flashpoint situations or trying out stress relieving activities or practising positive rather than negative self-talk.

ACTION STAGE

The action stage is when the new behaviour starts, when they employ what they have learned in the 'classroom' in the field. So the trainers hit tarmac, or the angry teen tries to interact with others without getting angry in the first place, or losing control of their anger.

MAINTENANCE AND RELAPSE PREVENTION

Maintenance and relapse prevention involves

incorporating the new behaviour over the long haul so it becomes permanent. Discouragement over occasional slips may halt the change process and result in the person giving up or may result in a 'recycling' through the stages of change. So some may enter a phase of precontemplation again. Others will re-enter the cycle at the contemplation stage, revisiting the reasons why they decided to make the change in the first place to be remotivated, to re-prepare and to try again. The frequency of relapse and recycling will vary from person to person but the cycle has to occur at least once fully (and most likely more) for a change to become completely established.

GETTING INTO THE CHANGE CYCLE

In helping teens to address their anger issues, it is therefore imperative that we recognise where they are in the process of change and don't seek to leap in with strategies and approaches before they are ready, before they have even contemplated change. If we do, it will only confirm our cluelessness in their minds and further switch them off to the idea of change.

For the most challenging teens, the ones that we bang our heads off the wall about, the issue is often that they are at the pre-contemplative stage and are utterly resistant to the idea of change. In which case, how do we get them to move from here onto the later stages?

In my experience the leap from pre-contemplative to contemplative is one of the biggest and most challenging to make, at least for us as their workers trying to help them make it! This is the point at which so many challenging young people get left behind and are labelled 'unworkable'.

It is not that they are unworkable, it is just that our approaches are unworkable for where they are on the cycle of change. We need to respect where they are on the cycle and work with that and through that if we are to help them set off down the road of change.

FROM RESISTANCE TALK TO CHANGE

So how do we practically make this work? How do we get them to stop and think about doing things differently without inadvertently bolstering their anti-change position? How do we get them to make that quantum leap from pre-contemplation to contemplation?

Pure and simply, we need to avoid doing the one thing that helps them to avoid acknowledging or addressing the issue- arguing. Even if there is no shouting or expletives, engaging in an argument or debate will likely get us nowhere in effecting change. Why? Because we are creating an environment where they can finely hone their arguments as to why they don't need to change (resistance talk), rather than doing exactly what we need them to do - exploring the idea of change (change talk).

RESISTANCE TALK

Resistance talk includes:

Statements that deny there is an issue to be dealt with:

'Get lost, I don't have an anger problem'

'Everyone else my age drinks. So I get a bit lairy. What's the problem?'

Statements about intentions not to change:

'If you think I'm going to listen to anything you've got

to say then you are mad. I'm fine as I am thanks. It's you with the problem.'

Statements about the advantages of the status quo:

'No-one messes with me, I'm the gangsta round here.'

'People know just to back off and leave me alone.'

'I go my own way, no one can stop me.'

'It's buzzin', pure buzzin''

Statements about the disadvantages of change:

'How the hell else am I supposed to get anyone to listen to me?'

'Everyone will think I've gone soft, a total pussy'.

'What am I supposed to do on a Friday night if I stop drinking? Might as well die, life would be so boring.'

Statements of pessimism about change:

'What's the point anyway? It'll make sod all difference to anything'

'I can't change. It's just the way I am.'

Non-engagement:

'Whatever'

'Huh?'

Silence, or change of subject.

Research has shown that with young people *the most vital*

indicator of change is a reduction in this kind of resistance talk (Bauer et al 2008). So the most important thing you can do to try and achieve change is to limit the amount of resistance talk a teen engages in. This means that you need to stop trying to argue the case for them to change, stop trying to persuade them, it will only encourage them to engage in this kind of talk.

Arguing against adult's opinions is a normal part of the teen developmental process. Developing a greater sense of autonomy is a vital part of the pathway to adulthood and the natural partner to this is a greater resistance to adult authority. By trying to tell or even persuade them why they need to change, they will perceive that you are limiting their personal freedoms (and their drive towards greater autonomy and adulthood) and are more likely to have a negative resistant response and to engage in resistance talk (Brehm 1966). The end result is that you both leave the interaction more convinced of your own rightness and nowhere near change, even if lipservice has been paid.

So what can you do if you can't argue the case for change with them? They need to see the other side of the debate. They're stuck in their own thinking. If they don't see the other side, surely they'll get nowhere?

Well yes, someone does need to present the arguments for change, someone does need to consider the pros and cons of continuing in the current behaviour and in trying out some new behaviour. And the best person for the job? The teen themselves. Your role is not to argue or debate with them. Your role is to help them argue their own case for change.

HELPING THEM MAKE THEIR OWN CASE FOR CHANGE

So how do you help them to argue their own case for change? How do you get round all the objections, the arguments, the resistance talk, the sheer bloody-minded opposition?

PUT THEM IN THE DRIVING SEAT

When beginning to try to get them to reconsider a behaviour, if you start off with a statement that conveys that you realise that they are in control of what they do and the decisions they make, and not you, then their ears will prick up. For most teens this is a radically different statement from the ones they are used to hearing from adults. They are far more used to being told how what they are doing is wrong and what they should be doing is x, y and z.

Once you have made their autonomy clear you can then explain how your interactions are going to work: 'I want to help you make the best decisions for you. I don't want to lay down the law, I don't want to tell you what to do. I just want to help you explore what's going on in your life at the moment and to really understand where you are coming from. I really want to explore together and understand you more so I can help you decide how you want to handle this situation.'

It's harder to argue with someone when they state that they want to listen to you and respect your right to choose. The most ardent resisters might still throw out resistance talk and continue to avoid addressing the issue. A classic would be, 'There is no poxy situation. Just get lost'. In which case, you will need to employ one of the other following strategies.

GET THEM TO TELL YOU HOW THEY SEE THE SITUATION

Whatever you do, don't tell them what you see the situation as being, e.g. drinking too much, being too aggressive etc. Even if it is well meant and framed helpfully like, 'I really want to help you with your over-drinking' or 'I really want to understand why you get so angry that you lose control so I can help you', all the teen will hear is that you are more interested in your own take on things than you are on listening to them. They'll try and avoid listening to you, will dig in their heels and will resistance-talk till the cows come home to avoid having to engage with you.

If you tell them how you perceive the situation you are also missing out on an opportunity to understand better how they view their behaviour and how much and what sort of work you need to do with them to get them to a place where they will contemplate change.

A straightforward way of getting them to tell you how they see the situation is to ask them an open-ended question about why they think they are having this conversation or are in this session with you: 'Why do you think you are here?' (If you have experienced further resistance as highlighted above, moving the conversation onto this question could be a way of moving the conversation on).

For example, with anger control issues, you might get the following answers and these will give you some indicator of their readiness for change:

- *'because you think I need anger management?'*

[They probably don't really think they have a problem, or if they do have some realisation they clearly don't think it is as big a problem as you do. Some way to go before ready to make a change]

- *'because the court said I had to'*

[I'm not really interested in change, I'm just here through coercion]

- *'because I've got a temper'*

[possibly receptive to idea of changing behaviour as owning the behaviour]

- *'I have no idea'*

[May just be nervous, may not be interested in engaging, or have no idea that their behaviour is a problem and therefore nowhere near change]

One simple question like this can allow a teen to express themselves and provides you with valuable information as to what they see the issues as being and how resistant to change they really are. Most importantly you avoid creating an argumentative environment that resistance talk thrives in, by avoiding putting words in their mouth.

AVOID USING THE TERM 'PROBLEM'

Don't refer to their situation or the issues in their lives as 'problems'. This will be perceived as judgmental. If they think you are judging them then they are more likely to clam up or to engage in resistance talk, arguing why they do not have a problem. Terms like 'situation', or 'issue' are far less negatively perceived.

RESPONDING TO RESISTANCE TALK

NEUTRALITY

Have you ever tried to argue with someone who refuses to argue with you? Have you ever tried to argue with someone who is really listening to you and trying to understand a situation from your perspective? It's virtually impossible.

So when they throw out resistance talk to try and get you to argue with them or to make you go away, disarm them by refusing to argue or debate with them. Go Swiss and take a neutral position.

The underlying ethos of *remaining neutral* or *rolling with resistance* is that it prevents interactions from going down a conversational dead end as occurs when a debate or argument ensues- you both get stuck down the entrenched viewpoint cul-de-sac. Instead if you keep the conversation flowing and constantly seek to elicit information from your teen, you can direct the conversation so that they end up providing themselves with their own arguments for change.

REFLECTION

The most important tool you have in maintaining your neutrality is the tool of reflection- reflecting back at them what they have said. It provides you with something to say when you don't know what to say, and particularly when you disagree with what they have said.

Rather than entering a debate with them where they end up giving arguments against change and being more resistant, you avoid challenging them and 'roll with the resistance'. By reflecting you end up using the young person's momentum to further explore their views and most importantly you keep the conversation going.

For example, if they state, "I wouldn't have smashed up my room if my stupid foster carer hadn't been such a cow." you can respond with, "You're upset with your foster carer" [reflects the emotion] or "The reason you smashed up your room is because of your foster carer" [restates their statement].

You aren't agreeing or disagreeing with them and thereby stalling the conversation. Instead, you are inviting them to say more.

It is often only when they hear what they have said reflected back to them that they can see for themselves that their thinking is confused, incomplete or contradictory. The use of carefully worded open-ended questions in light of their elaborations can also help them to think through their own thinking and move the conversation forward.

OPEN-ENDED QUESTIONS

Open-ended questions draw out far more information than closed questions and cause them to really reflect on their lives, their thoughts and their actions. They also can provide you with valuable information on what might motivate them to change.

For example, it is easy to see that the closed question, "Do you think your anger is a problem?" will garner far less reflection and information than the question, "What problems has your anger caused for you?"

In addition, closed questions can lead to a young person feeling like you are trying to trick them into accepting your way of thinking or a particular intervention or treatment. Open questions are far better for increasing internal motivation to change.

Open-ended questions can also provide opportunities for

you to neutrally present them with some additional generalised information. You can then enquire as to what they make of it, providing them with an opportunity to consider, in an unthreatening manner, how it relates to them.

For example, "Research has shown that alcohol increases the likelihood that someone who has a tendency to be angry anyway will become aggressive when provoked. What's your experience?"

(For more on this research see Parrott et al 2003).

REFRAMING STATEMENTS

In addition to reflections and open-ended questions, reframing of statements can also shift conversations from resistance to considering change. They essentially show that you are listening while simultaneously introducing the idea of change. This can be seen in the following examples:

> *Teachers are such a bunch of dicks. They are always on my case, always.'*

> 'Teachers are annoying you. (Emotive Reflection) I wonder if there is some way we can get them to give you more positive attention?' (Reframe)

> *'Well what did he expect? Get in my face like that and he has to expect me to lamp him one.'*

> 'So you feel he was winding you up (Emotive Reflection). What else might he have expected? Is there any other way you could have dealt with that?' (Reframe)

THE IMPORTANCE OF PURPOSE & DIRECTION

It is very easy for young people to coast in their sessions with you, to turn up, do the session, and leave again, turning off their thinking until the next session. This way the session is viewed as a discrete chunk of time and there is little continuity of thinking from one session to the next. So while they might appear to be engaging well they are not actually really any closer to contemplating change.

If they are to stand any chance of moving closer to contemplating change the thinking about change needs to infuse their thinking all through the week and not just when they are with you. They need to clearly see how what you do with them from one session to another is linked and be actively invited to think about it in-between sessions.

SUMMARISING

Clarity of purpose and direction can be achieved by summarising what has been said at the end of sessions. This helps to confirm what has been achieved and gives future discussion and action a direction. It also helps a young person to feel a little more in control of the whole process as they know where it is going and what is expected of them. Uncertainty should not be underestimated as a tool of disengagement.

Summaries should highlight the major discussion points, help to clarify any agreed action plan and help to confirm for both you and the young person why they have decided to take action and the consequences of following through and not following through. This should stimulate further thought on the part of the young person through the week.

Summaries also put emphasis on positive steps forward

that have been made that you wish to positively reinforce and affirm.

The following example shows how this can be achieved:

> "OK, so it looks like we're about out of time. We've been covering some of the things the court has stated we need to achieve in the coming weeks. You thought it would just be easier to get the drinking and drug assessment out of the way, and you've agreed to keep a drinking and drug use diary over the next week so we can both see how much you are using and whether we think this is an issue or not. We won't be able to cover this part of your order until you have done this and it would be great to look at this at the beginning of next session. Agreed? [Pause for response].
>
> You've said that you have some real mixed feelings about doing any anger management work. You're aware that it's one of your conditions but are worried it might be a waste of your time because you think your responses to certain situations are just what anyone else would do. We can revisit that next session if you want to take some time to think about it. [Pause for potential response].
>
> I know we've covered a lot in a short period of time, and I do appreciate your willingness to work with me and for coming on time today so we could get going on this. Is there anything else I need to know before we meet next week?"

AFFIRMATIONS

Affirmations help to reinforce positive behaviours and are progress markers along the road for both you and your teen. They also help build rapport, provide feedback and make positive behaviours more likely.

Affirmations can be given for something a young person has done, e.g. "Well done for getting here on time", or can point towards something admirable or interesting about the person, e.g. "You really look out for your sister don't you?". They can also increase a young person's appreciation of their own thinking skills. e.g. "How did you know that would work?".

It goes without saying that offering affirmations will build self-esteem, will further strengthen your relationship with them. They will help build trust and more open conversations will ensue which can only aid you in guiding them towards contemplating and achieving change.

PERSUASION OUT, PATIENCE IN

So if you have a teen who is resistant to the idea of change, don't try to argue or persuade them, it only encourages them to focus on why they don't want to change and to engage in resistance talk. Your focus instead should be on neutrally exploring their viewpoint and guiding them to think about reasons for change, what that change might look like and how it might be achieved.

Don't get me wrong. This approach is no easy or quick fix. For the most disengaged and the most resistant to change, you will need a truckload of patience. There will be no overnight cure.

The key to it all in my opinion is to stop being impatient, no matter how urgent the resolution of the issue might be. You need to take the time to listen to them, to explore ideas with them and endeavour to understand them more, to understand how they tick.

The best way to achieve this is by getting them to talk and being neutral helps you to sweep aside the biggest barrier to this- their fear that you are going to try and control them, make them do something they don't want to do, and force them to change. This is of particular importance for those teens with anger issues that stem from a deep drive to be in control. While this underlying issue will ultimately need to be addressed there is no need to put up barriers to addressing these issues before you've even started. Engagement and relationship building comes first and listening and exploring goes hand in hand with that.

Telling them what they should do because that seems like the quickest way to effect change is wholly counter-productive. The only person who can make the change is the teen themselves and engaging in debate or argument pushes them further away, not nearer to change. All you can do is guide them, provide them with helpful information and help them to understand themselves better so that they can make better decisions *for themselves.*

We need to guide them to a place where they begin to argue their own case for change. We are merely a provider of dots, they have to join them in their own time. Give them that time and that space. It's the best route and the only route to real lasting change.

The strategies described in this chapter are part of the Motivational Interviewing approach which emphasises the eliciting and strengthening of internal motivation for change. For more information on this method and appropriate techniques to use for each of the stages of change, visit:

www.teenagewhisperer.co.uk/teenanger

\-

MOVING ON

\-

WHEN YOU SEE MORE THAN YOU SEE: THE OTHER SIDE

When I walk my way through life with my head held high, I am not just walking along with a puffed up sense of pride or a performance of bravado. I am walking with my head up, eyes engaged, because I am freed from the shame, the burden, the manipulation, the performance, the raw emotion, the chains of my anger. I smile at you, I crack a joke. I see potential connection in people, not inevitable disconnection. I am living my life boldly, positively and outwardly rather than being controlled by inward fear and pain.

When I go and play basketball, I am not just shooting hoops. I am physically releasing pent up frustrations, stresses and life strains. I stand strong with my teammates around me who support me in the setup for a slam dunk and when I fall they'll offer me a hand.

I can share in the joy of achievement, in the joy of camaraderie, in the joy of being seen and valued by teammates and spectators, and the joy of knowing that they've got my back and I've got theirs.

When you see me with more friends, real friends, where give and take is the norm, where care resides, it's not just friendship you see, it's a ceding of control. I no longer feel the need to be in control of everything, the need to manipulate, because I am no longer afraid.

No longer afraid of the unknown, no longer expecting the worst in others, no longer feeling the need to protect myself from this with my manipulations. I am experiencing the natural ebb and flow, the surges, the calmness, the fluidity that are real relationships. And in those relationships I feel safer than when I thought I was in control.

When the flashpoints inevitably come, when I rush out the room, I am not being controlled by my anger, I am controlling it. I am giving myself and everyone else some mental space, lowering the emotional temperature so I can return at some point and actually communicate.

I know what my anger feels like, I know the fizzing blood, the pounding heart, the red mist descending, the sickness in my stomach and I know I have to calm down. I know what my anger does to my real voice, the damage it does to relationships. So I don't feed it, I don't let it win. I don't let it overwhelm me, overtake me. Instead I take it somewhere quiet, alone and I give my mind some time to catch up with the emotion and to take control. Perspective prevails.

I consider what I need to communicate and how to communicate it well, or consider whether I just need to move on. My mind controls me, not my raw emotion. And those around me learn that this is the best way to help me deal with this, and give me the breathing room when I need it.

When you hear me talk about my past, about my family,

about life experiences more easily than before with less raw emotion, it is not that the pain has gone, it is that I understand it and am not held captive by it. I have made connections between my anger and past hurts, how my behaviour has often been a set of learned responses to life circumstances, a survival strategy. With this knowledge I have been able to devise alternate strategies so I can break free from having to relive the pain every time I speak of it.

With this knowledge I understood more of why I have done what I have done, and I give myself a break. I learn to condemn my behaviour rather than the very essence of me and as a result no longer feel deep shame at what has happened to me because it is no longer the measure of me. Without this shame and condemnation of myself I have begun to rebuild my life, rebuild relationships, build new and better behaviours that tell more of who I am and less of what has gone before.

When you hear me telling people how I feel, I'm not just showing them like I used to, I'm using my real voice, telling them how and why I feel what I feel. I'm using a better route to having my needs met, using the best tools to maximise the chances of being heard and at the same time being considerate of others' needs. We might not agree, but I will be confident that at least I am communicating well.

When you see me being creative, expressing myself in music, art, writing, I am not just engaged in a hobby. I am engaged with myself. I am expressing myself positively, taking the time to consider, explore and connect with all the layers and perspectives of life, of others and myself. I am taking the time to make sense of it all.

When I go to school, to college, to work, regularly attending and engaging with anything, it's not just turning up, it's that I'm not hiding anymore. I'm not hiding from my painful emotions, I'm not paralysed with shame, I'm not angry with myself, I'm not depressed any more.

I'm not afraid to try because I'm not afraid of who I am. I'm not afraid of taking a chance. I'm not constantly condemning myself with an unrealistic expectation of perfection.

And once I'm not condemning myself I don't feel the need to lash out at others in frustration with myself, either as a conscious defence mechanism or as unbridled rage, so I have an opportunity to actually get stuff done rather than getting chucked out.

When you see me continuing to make progress, focusing on where I want to go in life, what I want to achieve, even when I continue to be verbally abused by others, even when I may still experience violence or neglect, you see that I no longer internalise the lies, the negativity that others wish to inflict upon me.

It still hurts, it still causes me pain, but I have the regular positive voices of others that I hold in my heart as truth instead. I can see the selfish motivations of others'. I see their pain and refuse to let them hold me in its grasp along with themselves. I refuse to do to others what they have done to me. I am not victim turned victimiser. I choose to live.

When someone goads me, prods me, tries to get a rise and I turn the other cheek, I am not a wimp, I am incredibly strong. I live with a peace in me, a deep experiential understanding that aggression robs the perpetrator as much as the victim. I do not let others' problems become my problems. I do not let the contagion of anger infect my soul.

When you see me muttering under my breath, I am not cursing you, I am practising the art of positive self-talk. I am battling to keep my grip, to not automatically go down the road of negative perception and interpretation. I am endeavouring to see the best and not the worst, to assess whether it is my perception or the truth that you or others are having a go.

I am striving to see, to really see and the more I practise, the better focus I get. There is a different track playing on loop in my head. The negative tracks of past experience, misconceptions and condemnation do not get airtime. My head is full of the positive tracks of future, of clarity, understanding and hope and that is what helps me keep my grip, helps me to make the right choices.

When I help others in some way, be it organised charity work, helping others in a support group, a class mate, a neighbour, a teacher, a youth worker, anyone, I am not just helping, I am gaining perspective. I'm opening my eyes to see that there are others with needs beyond my own which helps me control my emotions. I am gaining the real self-esteem from knowing that I am making a positive difference. And I am connecting with people in a positive way, spurring me on to keep that connection and keeping myself in check. As I really see others and connect, I see my anger less.

When I speak to the police, to social workers or get involved with organisations that look to protect others in ways that I was not, I am not seeking revenge, I am seeking justice. Justice, directly or indirectly for what was done to me. I am making my voice heard in a way that effects change.

Whether I ever receive direct justice depends on my willingness to speak and the desire of others to act. In both indirect and direct justice-seeking, the fact that I have spoken, stood up and been counted and heard is one of the keys to my letting go and moving on, healing. I have used the roots of my anger in the right way, to promote right action rather than wrong, and in so doing my anger has lost its sting, its negative hold over my life.

When you see me march forward with determination, I am not just marching forwards, I am marching away from the past. I am refusing to allow my future definition to be based on what has been, who I have been, my behaviour, and what others have done to me. I have accepted responsibility when responsibility has rested with me. I have placed responsibility at the feet of those who also need to take responsibility, whether they accept this or not. And because of this I do not walk in condemnation, I march in hope.

When I use words of kindness and encouragement to others, to my girl or my boy, to my family, to peers, to anyone who crosses my path, I am not just being kind. I have realised how my behaviour impacts others. I have learned respect. Respect for the needs of others, respect for myself. And I have learned what love and care really look like.

When you see me reach out and let people know I'm struggling, that life is tough, I'm not just relying on the support of others, I'm choosing not to rely on the ways of old. I'm choosing not to turn to drugs, to drink, to solvents, to violence or emotional explosions for a buzz, to any method in which the mental haze descends behind which I can hide.

Instead I'm engaging with my emotions, and engaging with others in order to cope. Better clarity of thinking, better decisions and ways forward can be seen. I am trusting others who even when not at their best, help me think and act more clearly than the methods of old ever did.

When you see any of these things or more, I have not just been changed by a formula, I have been helped to change by you. You saw me, you heard me, you fought to connect. Your compassion and your perseverance caught me. Your patience, your desire to understand and care for a nothing like me, helped me to realise I was something. Something worth listening to, something worth caring for, something worth trying to help to change. And so I paid attention, and so I listened to you. Listened as we explored my past, my life injuries and my life hopes. Listened as I tried out new ways of coping, of living life, of being me, of being some*body*. You saw me first, you saw me first and helped me to see and discover the real me.

REFERENCES

Bauer, J.S. et al (2008) 'Adolescent change language within a brief motivational intervention and substance use outcome', *Psychology of Addictive Behaviors*, 22:570-575

Brehm, J. W. (1966). *A theory of psychological reactance* (London:Academic Press)

Parrott, D.J., Zeichner, A., Stephens, D. (2003) 'Effects of Alcohol, Personality, and Provocation on the Expression of Anger in Men: A Facial Coding Analysis', *Alcoholism: Clinical and Experimental Research*, 27:937-945

Prochaska, J. O. & C. C. DiClemente (1983) 'Stages and processes of self-change of smoking: Toward an integrative model of change', *Journal of Consulting and Clinical Psychology* 51(3): 390-395

Siebenthal, P. (2012) 'In My Shoes', *Aspienaut blog*, 8 March 2012, *http://aspienaut.tumblr.com/post/18944099081/in-my-shoes*

Tobias, C. U. (2002) *You Can't Make Me [But I Can Be Persuaded]: Strategies for Bringing Out the Best in Your Strong-Willed Child* (Colorado Springs: WaterBrook Press)

Yurgelun-Todd, D. (2002) Frontline interview "Inside the Teen Brain" on PBS.org. *http://www.pbs.org/wgbh/pages/frontline/shows/teenbrain/interviews/todd.html*

SAM ROSS

BSc, Msc, Msc, Cert EP (YJ)

Sam Ross, popularly known as the 'Teenage Whisperer', is passionate about connecting with and helping the most challenging, disengaged and troubled teens to turn their lives around. She has worked in both educational and youth justice settings, both with young people and their parents or carers. Really understanding teens is the beginning, middle and end of her work and she helps professionals and parents achieve this through her website, books and training.

To find out more about her work, to read her blog and to connect with her and other like-minded professionals please visit:

www.teenagewhisperer.co.uk

@Teen_Whisperer

www.facebook.com/teenagewhisperer

12206267R00101

Printed in Great Britain
by Amazon.co.uk, Ltd.,
Marston Gate.